INSIDERS' GUIDE®

FUN WITH THE FAMILY™ SERIES

DISCARD

fun WITH the Family™

OHIO

HUNDREDS OF IDEAS FOR DAY TRIPS WITH THE KIDS

KHRISTI S. ZIMMETH

SIXTH EDITION

INSIDERS' GUIDE®

GUILFORD, CONNECTICUT
AN IMPRINT OF THE GLOBE PEQUOT PRESS

The prices, rates, and hours listed in this guidebook
were confirmed at press time. We recommend, however, that you
call establishments to obtain current information before traveling.

To buy books in quantity for corporate use
or incentives, call **(800) 962–0973, ext. 4551,**
or e-mail **premiums@GlobePequot.com.**

INSIDERS' GUIDE®

Text design by Nancy Freeborn and Linda Loiewski
Maps by Rusty Nelson © Morris Book Publishing, LLC
Spot photography throughout © Photodisc and © RubberBall Productions

ISSN: 1539-2872
ISBN-13: 978-0-7627-4034-5
ISBN-10: 0-7627-4034-5

Manufactured in the United States of America
Sixth Edition/First Printing

For my family—John, Nate, and Claire—the best
traveling companions a mom could ask for.

OHIO

Contents

Acknowledgments

My thanks to all who contributed to the writing of the six editions of this book, especially the incredibly organized folks at the Ohio Division of Travel and Tourism; Mike Urban at Globe Pequot, who got the ball rolling; and Jane Merryman and Justine Rathbun, my editors, who made sure it all made sense.

Introduction

Ohio has long been a favored family playground. With an incredible state park system—arguably one of the best in the country—folks lucky enough to live in or near the Buckeye State have found it hard to leave their own backyard when they travel. And why should they?

These days, residents from neighboring states are discovering what Ohio residents have known all along: Ohio truly is the heart of it all.

I've scoured the state with my family (son, Nate, thirteen; daughter, Claire, ten; and husband, John) to find new attractions, updated information, and more. We've divided the state by regions and included all the top spots, and a few off-the-beaten-path discoveries as well. There's more than enough to keep you busy. Because definitions of "fun" vary widely, I've tried to include something for everyone.

To make this book more user-friendly, a dollar sign has been used instead of a numerical rate for lodgings, restaurants, and attractions. Prices change often, so if you're counting on a certain rate, be sure to call ahead. Please note that the price ranges represent admission costs for both adults and children. I've also included Web sites whenever possible to help your planning process.

Rates for Lodging

$	up to $50
$$	$51 to $75
$$$	$76 to $99
$$$$	$100 and up

Rates for Attractions

$	up to $5.00 per person
$$	$5.01 to $10.00 per person
$$$	$10.01 to $20.00 per person
$$$$	more than $20 per person

Rates for Restaurants

$	most entrees less than $10
$$	most $10 to $15
$$$	$16 to $20
$$$$	most more than $20

Note, too, that the Ohio Department of Travel and Tourism is one of the best-run such agencies in the country. I encourage you to use them in planning trips and as an on-the-road resource. They're at (800) BUCKEYE (282–5393) or www.discoverohio.com. Park information is available at (800) ATAPARK (282–7275) or www.atapark.com, also a useful site.

We've had a great time in Ohio. We hope your family does, too. I'd love to hear from you about your favorites and incorporate them into the next edition.

It Happened Here First!

Most schoolchildren are familiar with famous firsts by persons born in Ohio—although the actual events took place elsewhere—such as the world's first successful flight in an airplane by Orville and Wilbur Wright or the invention of the incandescent bulb by Thomas Edison. Here are some other "Ohio firsts":

The first major league professional baseball team, the Cincinnati Reds, was organized in 1866.

The American Pro Football Association, direct forerunner of the National Football League, was founded in Canton on September 17, 1920. The Pro Football Hall of Fame is still located in Canton.

The first gorilla born in captivity was born at the Columbus Zoo on December 22, 1956.

The first dental school in the world was started by John M. Harris in Bainbridge in 1828.

Ohio University, founded in 1804 in Athens, was the first university in Ohio and the Northwest Territory.

The nation's first interracial, coeducational college was founded in Oberlin in 1833.

In 1841 Oberlin became the first school in the nation to award college degrees to women.

The first kindergarten in America was established by German settlers in Columbus in 1838.

The first chewing gum patent was issued to William Semple of Mount Vernon in 1869.

The first hot dog was made by Harry M. Stevens of Niles in 1904.

Soda jerk Letty Lally of Foeller's Drug Store made the first banana split in Columbus in 1904.

OhioFastFacts

Ohio has one of the best-run tourism offices in the country. Don't miss the opportunity to take advantage of it. One call or Web site visit will bring your family loads of brochures, magazines, and special offers to use in planning your Ohio vacation—and your kids can use the stuff later to put together their scrapbooks. Here's where to get the goods:

General Information

Ohio Department of Development
Division of Travel and Tourism
Box 1001
Columbus, OH 43216-0101
(800) BUCKEYE (282–5393)
www.discoverohio.com

National Forest Information

Forest Supervisor
Wayne National Forest
219 Columbus Road
Athens, OH 45701-1399
(740) 592–6644
www.dnr.state.oh.us/forestry

Recreation Information

Division of Parks and Recreation
Department of Natural Resources
2045 Morse Road
Columbus, OH 43229
(614) 265–6561
www.ohiostateparks.org

Fishing, Hunting, and Wildlife Information

Division of Wildlife
Department of Natural Resources
1840 Belcher Drive
Columbus, OH 43224-1329
(800) 945–3543
www.dnr.state.oh.us

Attractions Key

The following is a key to the icons found throughout the text.

SWIMMING		FOOD	
BOATING / BOAT TOUR		LODGING	
HISTORIC SITE		CAMPING	
HIKING / WALKING		MUSEUMS	
FISHING		PERFORMING ARTS	
BIKING		SPORTS/ATHLETIC	
AMUSEMENT PARK		PICNICKING	
HORSEBACK RIDING		PLAYGROUND	
SKIING/WINTER SPORTS		SHOPPING	
PARK		PLANTS / GARDENS / NATURE TRAILS	
ANIMAL VIEWING		FARMS	

Northwest Ohio

Northwest Ohio is a patchwork quilt of many colors. It's home to historic small towns and big, industrial cities, as well as the gateway to the state's famed Lake Erie playground and some of the best walleye fishing in the world. You'll find attractions to suit nature lovers and nostalgia buffs, train aficionados and thrill seekers. And all throughout this corner of Ohio you'll find that special brand of friendliness that will be a hallmark of your family's travels and a long-lasting memory of your time in the Buckeye State.

Khristi's
TopPicks for fun in Northwest Ohio

1. The scream machines at Cedar Point, Sandusky

2. Riding the high-wire bike at COSI, Toledo

3. Just hangin' out in the relaxing Lake Erie Islands

4. The hippoquarium at the Toledo Zoo

5. Water sports and more at Maumee State Park, Oregon; indoor water sports at the Great Bear Lodge in Sandusky

6. Far-out adventures at the Neil Armstrong Air and Space Museum, Wapakoneta

NORTHWEST OHIO

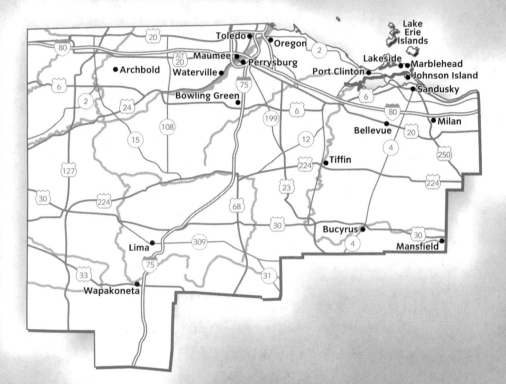

Toledo • • Oregon
80
20
Maumee 2
Archbold Perrysburg Lakeside Marblehead
Waterville Port Clinton Johnson Island
6 75 Sandusky
2 Bowling Green 6 80
24 199 Milan
108 Bellevue 20
15 4 250
12
127 Tiffin
224 23 224
30 224
68
30
309 Bucyrus Mansfield
Lima 4 30
75
33 31
Wapakoneta

Toledo

Toledo almost ended up as part of Michigan, its near northern neighbor. During the Toledo War of 1835–36, it was claimed by both states. When the battle was over, the city was annexed to Ohio, and the Northern Peninsula became part of Michigan.

It's not hard to see why it was in such demand. Today fun and friendly Toledo is a thriving industrial city and one of the world's busiest freshwater ports. Promenade Park, a peaceful, landscaped setting along the Maumee River, is still a favorite spot for watching the huge freighters and hardworking towboats that call the Great Lakes home. It's also the venue for weekend festivals, sailboat regattas, rowing competitions, powerboat races, and other colorful waterside entertainment. Recently, more and more businesses and attractions have opened, giving downtown's waterfront a new liveliness. The latest is the Toledo Mud Hens, who moved to a new downtown stadium in 2003. All this adds up to one kid-friendly city. Toledo was even rated number one for families in Ohio according to a recent survey by Zero Population Growth.

Willis B. Boyer (ages 5 and up)

26 Main Street; (419) 936–3070. Open May 1 through October 31 daily, November 1 through April 30 Wednesday through Sunday by appointment. $

Freighter fans won't want to miss a visit to the *Willis B. Boyer,* docked in the heart of downtown at International Park. The massive 617-foot ship was launched in 1911 and retired in 1980. Today it depicts how the largest, most modern ship on the Great Lakes looked in its heyday. It has been refurbished as a tribute to the city's rich port heritage and to the many freighters that continue to travel these waterways. Don't miss the chance to take your kids' picture at the wheel.

Tony Packo's Cafe (all ages)

1902 Front Street; (419) 691–6054; www.tonypacko.com. $$

Freighter watching make you hungry? Head across the river for a little sustenance, Toledo style. Your kids may have never heard of *M*A*S*H*'s Corporal Klinger, but it won't matter once they're chowing on a chili sundae with a side of taco chips at Tony Packo's Cafe, one of the city's top attractions and much more than just a place to eat. Native son Jamie Farr, better known as the quirky, cross-dressing Corporal Klinger, grew up in this neighborhood bordering the river and brought this Hungarian-style eatery to national attention when he starred on the long-running hit series in the 1970s and 1980s. Farr raved about the eatery during seven different episodes of *M*A*S*H* and still visits a few times a year to get his fill of Packo's chili dogs.

The cafe had been a local favorite for decades before it was "discovered" by *M*A*S*H* audiences. Tony Packo Sr. opened the unassuming storefront restaurant, then just a bar and a few tables, in 1933 with a few old Hungarian family recipes. It soon caught on, and the cafe expanded into adjacent buildings as business grew.

Tony Jr. has added family entertainment, including magicians on weekends and a great children's menu with classics such as peanut butter and jelly, grilled cheese, and American-style hot dogs. Visitors of all ages still opt for the house specialties: stuffed cabbage, with almost a pound of meat wrapped in a cabbage leaf and smothered with tomato sauce; tangy chicken paprikash; or the signature chili dog, with sausage and Packo's famous chili.

That chili dog and its fans are memorialized throughout the restaurant. Legend has it that Packo's wife started the tradition when Burt Reynolds visited in 1973. Seeking something more original for his autograph, she had him sign a hot dog bun. Today Reynolds's signature is just one of hundreds on the walls, from celebrities such as musician Frank Zappa ("Great Buns") to Roseanne Barr, Steve Martin, Bill Cosby, Kevin Costner, and even Margaret Thatcher and former President Bill Clinton.

Toledo Museum of Art (ages 3 and up)

2455 Monroe Street; (419) 255–8000, (800) 644–6862; www.toledomuseum.org. Open 10:00 A.M. to 4:00 P.M. Tuesday to Thursday, 10:00 A.M. to 10:00 P.M. Friday, 10:00 A.M. to 4:00 P.M. Saturday, and 11:00 A.M. to 5:00 P.M. Sunday. Free.

Glass figures prominently at the Toledo Museum of Art. Museums can be stuffy and lifeless—or they can be like this lively arts institution. Visit on a Saturday and you're likely to encounter young aficionados everywhere: lounging outside near a larger-than-life abstract sculpture such as Mel Kendrick's *Sculpture No. 4,* sketching in the galleries, or taking a class or workshop at the adjacent art school.

Local residents are justifiably proud of this small but choice museum. All the big names are here: El Greco, Rubens, van Gogh, Picasso, Monet, Matisse—and more. Founded in 1901 with funds from the Libbey Glass family, its collection today spans 5,000 years and almost as many cultures. Not surprisingly, the museum has one of the best collections of art glass found anywhere in the world. Airy and light-filled, it's a pleasure to explore.

A $15 million face-lift was done in honor of the museum's recent centennial. A visible addition is a life-size $4.1 million sculpture of a stegosaurus, centerpiece of a sculpture garden. The museum has also attracted a number of blockbuster-style traveling exhibits, including Eternal Egypt: Masterworks of Ancient Art from the British Museum and Star Wars: The Magic of Myth.

A good way to get acquainted is to catch the four-and-a-half-minute video shown continuously in the lobby. After that, head past the large, colorful Matisse cutout of

Amazing Ohio Facts

Ohio's motto is "With God, All Things Are Possible."

Apollo, made from radiant shards of blues, oranges, and reds, and take the stairs to the second floor, where you'll find the majority of the permanent galleries.

Indiana Jones wannabes won't want to miss the Egyptian room, where a well-preserved mummy from the ancient city of Akmin dates from the Ptolemaic period (304–30 B.C.) and fascinates amateur archaeologists of all ages. Would-be warriors can press a button in the African gallery and listen to a circa 1900–25 wooden slit drum pound out messages or imagine what it would be like to wear one of the heavy and intricately beaded headdresses from Zaire. Is surrealism more your style? If so, challenge your kids to see how many different tools they can find incorporated into Jim Dine's *The Crommelynck Gate* (1983).

One of the best things about visiting a museum is discovering how people lived in other times. Portraits of children—from Dutch painter Carel Fabritius's *The Happy Child* (1645) to Abbott Handerson Thayer's *Portrait of Helen Sears* (1891–92)—provide grounds for studying both similarities and differences.

My kids enjoy visiting on Friday for the museum's "It's Friday" series, which features food, fun, entertainment, and a kids' drop-in studio where pint-size Picassos can create their own masterpieces. Thursday and Sunday are also good days to visit, when the popular, hands-on Family Center offers costumes, games, books, puppets, and a "design-your-own gallery" hunt.

Center of Science & Industry (COSI) (all ages)

1 Discovery Way; (419) 244–COSI; www.cositoledo.org. Open 10:00 A.M. to 5:00 P.M. Monday to Saturday and noon to 5:00 P.M. Sunday. $$

Back downtown, head for one of the latest additions to Toledo's waterfront—the Center of Science and Industry, better known as COSI. This hands-on, interactive museum—one of the biggest things to hit Toledo in years—focuses on the wonders of the world of science and includes a number of special displays that trace the city's history, including glassmaking and automotive exhibits. The museum is an outpost of the popular museum in Columbus and has attracted more than two million visitors since it opened in 1997.

There's something here for everyone. My kids (even Nate, the sophisticated thirteen-year-old) love the wet and wild adventures in the Water, Water Everywhere area, where they can get their hands wet piloting a boat or playing in bubbles. Claire, almost ten, loves playing doctor in the kid-size clinic and scampering up the full-size tree house. Nate now would rather play virtual basketball or hop on one of those large foot-operated piano keys. My husband and I always marvel at the miniature tornado and dare each other to jump on the high-wire bike (neither of us had taken up the challenge until . . . see Dare You!, page 6). There's also a number of changing traveling exhibitions from around the United States. The most recent was Dinosaurs of the Deep and The Science of Big Machines.

Afterward, don't miss the nicely stocked shop where you can pick up lots of fun and educational goodies, and the on-site cafe, which looks out over the river.

Dare **You!**

I've never gone over Niagara Falls in a barrel or done anything truly crazy, but I like to think I'll rise to a challenge when it's presented to me. That's how I found myself teetering on a bicycle suspended on a high wire during a visit to Toledo's Center of Science and Industry (COSI). My then six-year-old, Nate, goaded me into it. I almost changed my mind a million times while I waited in line, but I was glad afterward, despite a lingering feeling of seasickness, when another little boy who had watched me turned to Nate and said, "Hey, your mom's pretty cool!" Darn right, I thought.

Toledo Zoo (all ages)

2700 Broadway; (419) 385–5721; www.toledozoo.org. Open 10:00 A.M. to 5:00 P.M. daily in summer; 10:00 A.M. to 4:00 P.M. otherwise. $$

A favorite spot for viewing the wonders of the natural world is the Toledo Zoo, located a few miles from downtown. This respected zoo, founded in 1899, houses more than 3,000 animals representing 525 species on fifty-one acres. Clever BETCHA DIDN'T KNOW signs posted throughout give unusual facts and figures about zoo inhabitants. The zoo was voted one of the top five in the country by Microsoft's *Zoo Tycoon* game players.

Ever come nose to nose with a hippo? You will at the world's only "Hippoquarium," voted one of the ten best animal exhibits in the country by *USA Today* Weekend. Two Nile hippos appear almost graceful as they dog-paddle around an underwater viewing area. Visitors have witnessed three live underwater births since the attraction opened in 1986. The 8-foot-deep pool holds 360 gallons of water that is pumped through four 8,000-gallon filters every ninety minutes.

Go on safari in the African Savannah, where you can explore the naturally landscaped environment while searching for lions, giraffes, rhinos, meerkats (they look something like gophers), and other animals that roam freely. Watch the pandas wash themselves like cats. Marvel at the tree-climbing koalas. The Toledo Zoo is one of only twelve zoos in the United States to permanently exhibit these cuddly animals.

The zoo takes its educational mission seriously—but not at the expense of fun. Your kids won't care that the Diversity of Life exhibit won a Significant Achievement Award from the American Zoological Association, but they won't be able to keep their hands off the exhibit's microscopes and magnifying glasses that allow them to examine the delicate wings of a tiny blue butterfly or watch tarantulas crawling around their well-fortified box.

Newer exhibits include an expanded aviary with more than 300 birds; a reopened primate forest, home to a variety of monkeys, apes, and gibbons; and a new bald eagle habitat. In 2000 the zoo increased its exhibit size by 50 percent, including an extensive Arctic habitat featuring polar bears and seals, among others. Arctic Encounter is the zoo's largest exhibit, housing seals and polar bears in their natural habitat. A new wolf exhibit opened in late 2002. An expansive Africa exhibit opened in 2004 and is the largest, most ambitious project in the zoo's 107-year history. The five-acre exhibit is home to Masai giraffes, Grant's zebras, impalas, wildebeests, and the African wild dog, considered one of the most endangered carnivore species in Africa. You could easily spend the day exploring the three distinct exhibit areas, including a town, a village, and a bush wilderness area.

My family's favorites: the reptile building, where a huge Burmese python holds court among other lesser reptiles; the friendlier species in the Children's Zoo, including Tony the llama, Buckie the horse, and Nugget the Vietnamese potbellied pig; and the extensive Kingdom of the Apes, where you can watch the wonderful antics of orangutans, chimps, and gorillas.

If the animal kingdom loses its appeal, head for the old-fashioned carousel, the playground (where kids can pretend to be a butterfly, a spider, or a warthog), or rest weary feet with a ride on the tiny red train that circles the zoo grounds. Or head for the Elephant's Trunk Gift Shop, where you can stock up on souvenirs of your visit, with wares from T-shirts and rubber animals to penguin-shaped sidewalk chalk and even Zoo Doo, organic compost made from animal droppings.

Don't leave without having a bite in the Carnivore Cafe. Dedicated in 1927 as the Carnivora Building, it was once home to the zoo's primates and large cats. Now you're the species behind bars as you nosh on hamburgers, hot dogs, and other deli-style snacks in the same cages that once housed the zoo's largest animals.

Toledo Botanical Gardens (ages 5 and up) 🍁
5403 Elmer Drive; (419) 936–2986; www.toledogarden.org. Open 8:30 A.M. to 5:30 P.M. Free.

Beautiful blooms can be found at the Toledo Botanical Gardens, considered by many to be among the best in the state. This picturesque sixty-two-acre setting of meadows and gardens boasts fragrant herbs, roses, and colorful wildflowers. Browse in artists' galleries or peruse the many tempting offerings in the gardens' gift shop. Special events for families include cafe concerts and the popular Ghosts in the Garden program.

Stranaham Arboretum (ages 6 and up) 🍁
4131 Tantera Drive; (419) 841–1007; www.arboretum.utoledo.edu. Free.

The Stranaham Arboretum, part of the University of Toledo, also has gorgeous grounds to stroll through and more than forty-seven beautiful acres that entice aspiring green thumbs. Among the highlights are more than 2,000 woody plants representing 450 genera, including 54 maple species, and 48 varieties of fragrant, flowering crab apple. It's a great place to introduce your older kids to the natural world.

Information, **Please**

Although it's always a good idea to gather information before a trip, a stop at one of the various information centers across the state will reveal a wealth of brochures, accommodation ideas, and other useful literature. Once I even picked up a packet of native wildflower seeds to plant in my Michigan garden, a nice reminder of my Ohio stay. Another plus: A lot of them have bathrooms and picnic areas, useful stops for families on the move.

Locations include Interstate 90 westbound near Conneaut; Interstate 71 north and southbound near Lebanon; Interstate 80 westbound near Hubbard; Interstate 70 westbound near St. Clairsville; Interstate 77 northbound near Marietta; Interstate 75 north and southbound near Bowling Green; Interstate 70 eastbound near Gettysburg; Interstate 70 westbound at the U.S. Air Force Museum in Dayton; U.S. Highway 23 southbound between Wakefield and Lucasville; and the westbound Ohio Turnpike near New Springfield.

Information centers are open daily except Thanksgiving, Christmas, and New Year's Day.

Arawanna Belle (all ages) ⬠

International Park; (419) 691–7447. Call for ticket information and current prices.

Ever wanted to ride a paddle wheeler? Here's your chance. The *Arawanna Belle* is a true stern-wheeler driven by an authentic paddle wheel. She offers lunch or dinner cruises on the Maumee River as well as frequent Murder Mystery Cruises. The *Arawanna II* (419–255–6200) offers river tours of Maumee, Perrysburg, and Toledo from Rossford City Marina in suburban Rossford.

Northcoast Nauticals, Inc. (ages 5 and up)

1501 Monroe Street; (419) 243–7037; www.lighthousesbymurphy.com. Call for tour information. Free.

In summer this is the place to watch a miniature masterpiece being created right before your eyes. You'll ooh and aah as sculptors turn a plain piece of wood into an intricately carved lighthouse. This craft shop lets you experience wood-turning demonstrations and offers tours of the place, where more than 272 different lighthouses have been duplicated. An adjacent retail area sells nautical novelties and mini versions of your favorite Great Lakes lighthouse.

Sandpiper Canal Boat (all ages) ⊕

2144 Fordway; (419) 537–1212; www.sandpiperboat.org. Prices vary with tour chosen.

Stow away on this one-hundred-passenger canal boat and cruise up the Maumee River past elegant estates and yacht clubs or downriver toward Lake Erie. Besides public rides, which include port tours, fall-color cruises, and sunset and city lights cruises, the boat offers the fun and always popular Halloween Boat Rides for kids.

Schedel Arboretum and Gardens (all ages) ✸

19255 West Portage River Road; (419) 862–3182; www.schedel-gardens.org. Open Monday through Saturday from 10:00 A.M. to 4:00 P.M. and Sunday noon to 4:00 P.M. from April 15 to October 31. $

Looking for a serene place in the city? These beautiful Japanese gardens come complete with torii, waterfalls, pools, lanterns, bridges, and a pagoda. Stroll through rose, perennial, iris, lily pool blue, butterfly, and other gardens; join a guided group tour of the grounds and adjacent mansion; or just wander through the lushly landscaped arboretum, home to a variety of rare species from many lands.

Toledo Metroparks (all ages) ⚶ ✸

Twelve parks throughout metropolitan Toledo; (419) 407–9700; www.toledometro parks.com.

Nature-loving families know that the Toledo Metroparks are some of the best spots around for getting back to the basics. Twelve nature parks, each with its own features, offer sand dunes, horseback riding, pedal boats, and more. Parks are located throughout the Toledo area and are open dawn to dusk. One of the best is the Miami and Erie Canal Restoration area at Providence Metropark, where your family can take a trip back in time to the canal days of the nineteenth century. Rides on the canal boats feature mule-drawn transportation, historical interpreters, and more.

Where to Eat

Cousino's Navy Bistro, 26 Main Street; (419) 697–6289. Among a handful of new restaurants on the water, it has a wide variety of entrees for all ages. $–$$

Muer's Seafood, 1435 Baronial Plaza Drive; (419) 866–8877. A branch of the popular Detroit-based Muer seafood franchise with a nice, varied children's menu and a large outdoor patio popular with families in season. $$

Spaghetti Warehouse, 42 South Superior Street; (419) 255–5038. Family-focused chain in city's Warehouse District has lots of pasta pleasers. $–$$

Tony Packo's Cafe (see pages 3–4).

Where to Stay

Courtyard by Marriott, 1435 East Mall Drive, Holland; (419) 866–1001. A nice, budget choice, this well-run, 149-room hotel features a pool, sauna, spacious rooms, and a family-friendly breakfast bar. $

Maumee Bay State Park (see Oregon, page 13).

Wyndham Toledo, 2 Seagate/Summit Street; (419) 241–1411. Conveniently located downtown adjacent to COSI, with an indoor pool, restaurant, and game room. Most rooms have coffeemakers, which is nice for parents who have a hard time getting going in the morning. $$

For More Information

Greater Toledo Convention & Visitors Bureau, 401 Jefferson Avenue, Toledo 43604-1067; (800) 243–4667, (419) 321–6404; www.toledocvb.com.

Maumee

Toledo Mud Hens (ages 5 and up)
406 Washington Street; for tickets call (419) 725–HENS (4367) or (800) 736–9520; www.mudhens.com. $$–$$$

If you've ever sat through nine endless innings of major-league baseball and wondered what happened to the kind of game you remember from your childhood, look no further than the Toledo Mud Hens, who play from April through September in a downtown stadium that opened in 2002. Stars may argue about contracts and endorsements, but back in the minor leagues, you'll still hear old-fashioned cries of "Play ball!"

This is the life chronicled in the hit movie *Bull Durham.* The stadiums are smaller, and fans can get box seats for just a few bucks. You're up close to the action, and you never know when a pop-up may come your way.

The Mud Hens are a Detroit Tigers farm team and are growing in popularity. In 2004 attendance jumped from 47,000 to more than 590,000. Attendance grew again in 2005, thanks in part to an amazing "Worst to First" turnaround. In fact, Toledo now ranks as ninth best minor league market. Part of the International League, they step up to the plate against such rivals as the Charlotte Knights (affiliated with the Florida Marlins), the Columbus Clippers (New York Yankees), the Pawtucket Red Sox (Boston Red Sox), and the Richmond Braves (Atlanta Braves). Their nickname has been voted the most popular in minor-league baseball.

What's a **Mud Hen?**

According to the team's Web site, a mud hen is a marsh bird with short wings and long legs often found in—surprise—marshes or swamps. They're also known as rails or coots. Who knew?

Besides all the regularly scheduled fun, there are special events such as Disco Night, Martian Antenna Night, Friendly's Muddy's Birthday Bash (in honor of Muddy, the Mud Hens' mascot), and Fright Night. There's also the annual Detroit Tigers/Toledo Tussle, complete with a baseball card show, held each July.

Wolcott House Museum Complex (ages 4 and up)

1031 River Road; (419) 893–9602. Open 1:00 to 4:00 P.M. **Wednesday through Sunday, April through December. $; children under six** free.

Old-fashioned fun of a different kind can be had at the Wolcott House Museum Complex on River Road. The six restored buildings—including a furnished, circa 1836 Federal-style house; a log cabin; a train depot; a farmhouse; and an 1840s Greek Revival–style home—offer a picture of what family life was like in the Maumee Valley in the years leading up to the Civil War.

Butterfly House (all ages)

11455 Obee Road, Whitehouse; (419) 877–2733; www.butterfly-house.com. **Open 10:00 A.M. to 5:30 P.M. Monday through Saturday; noon to 5:00 P.M. Sunday. Adults $$, children four to twelve and seniors $.**

A great place to stop in the Toledo area is the Butterfly House, part of the Obee Road Garden Center. Owners Duke and Martha Wheeler visited similar attractions around the country before opening their house in 2000. The facility was built with the idea of developing beautiful gardens in a controlled environment to exhibit North American butterflies. Families can wander through on self-guided tours and enjoy the more than 400 free-flying butterflies. A favorite of area schoolchildren, it also specializes in helping Ohio gardeners develop their own butterfly habitats. Special seasonal events include annual releases in summer.

Archbold

Sauder Farm and Craft Village (ages 4 and up)

22611 Highway 2; (419) 446–2541, (800) 590–9755; www.saudervillage.com. **Open 10:00 A.M. to 5:00 P.M. Tuesday through Saturday and 1:00 to 5:00 P.M. Sunday, mid-April through late October. Adults $$$, children ages six to sixteen $$, children under six** free.

Homage to the past is also paid at the Sauder Farm and Craft Village, off Highway 2 in nearby Archbold. Explore what life in mid-1800s rural Ohio was like by watching blacksmiths, potters, and glassblowers practice their arts at this fascinating living-history complex dedicated to fine all-American craftsmanship. With more than thirty buildings clustered around a central axis, you can easily spend a full day exploring here. A new permanent exhibit, Natives and Newcomers, Ohio in Transition 1803–1839, was added in 2003.

The pace is slow and the staff is friendly. Don't miss the extensive quilt shop, the general store (with lots of old-fashioned penny candy for little sweet tooths), or the simple but delicious lunches offered year-round at the country-style Barn Restaurant (yes, it was a real barn). Lighter fare can be had at the delicious Doughbox Bakery. Popular weekend events in season include fiddlers' contests, a doll show and sale in August, apple-butter making in September, and a whittlin' and woodcarvin' show in October. There's also a handy, thirty-seven-site adjacent campground.

Where to Stay and Eat

Home Restaurant, 218 North Defiance Street; (419) 445–6411. Home-cooked specials have been an area staple since 1912. $

Sauder Heritage Inn, Highway 2; (419) 445–6408. Thirty-four rooms are furnished with a friendly country style. Adjacent to Sauder Farm and Village. The popular Barn Restaurant (419–445–2231) is also located here and is a family favorite because of its huge salad bar, popular buffet, and kids' menu. $–$$

For More Information

Archbold Chamber of Commerce, (419) 445–2222.

Perrysburg

Fort Meigs (ages 5 and up) 🏛

2900 West River Road; (419) 874–4121, (800) 283–8916; www.fortmeigs.org. Open Wednesday through Saturday 9:30 A.M. to 5:00 P.M., Sunday noon to 5:00 P.M. during summer, weekends the rest of the year. The museum is open year-round. $

The land south of Toledo is also home to reconstructed Fort Meigs, the largest wooden-walled fortification in America. The sounds of fifes and drums and the smell of gunpowder transport visitors of all ages back to the time of the War of 1812, when the fort was built. Constructed by Gen. William Henry Harrison (later President Harrison) in 1813, it defended the area then known as Ohio Country against two sieges by the British and was used as a staging point for the retaking of Detroit and the invasion of Canada.

The reconstruction, begun in 1865, re-creates the stockade as it looked during the first British siege of 1813. The fort's seven blockhouses appear as they did then, with 2-foot-thick walls, 4-inch-deep window and cannon-port shutters, and white-washed interior walls. Several buildings contain fascinating exhibits and dioramas on the War of 1812, the fort's reconstruction, and the lives of the soldiers who were garrisoned here during the war.

Kids can view a six-pound cannon and the implements used to fire it and peer out of the second-floor gun ports, where soldiers took aim at a foreign enemy. On the Grand Battery, you can stand where General Harrison did when he watched as members of the Kentucky militia were trapped and taken prisoner on the other side of the Maumee River. On the Grand Parade, you can almost hear the barking of the sergeant as you imagine soldiers receiving their orders for the day, obtaining their rations, or going about their daily work.

Cannon demonstrations are held hourly and are a favorite of young military fans. Special events include reenactments, military encampments, and summer commemorative weekends. A new visitor center was added in 2003, and many exhibits were refurbished in time for the season.

Oregon

Maumee Bay State Park (all ages) 🕸️ 🌊 🏛️ 🍁

1750 Park Road, #2; (419) 836–1466, (800) AT–A–PARK (282–7275) for reservations; www.maumeebayresort.com. Free.

Had enough history for a while? When you're ready for some sun and surf (or, depending on the season, some snow and cross-country skiing), follow the sandy shores of Lake Erie to Maumee Bay State Park. Ohio is well known for its seventy-two excellent state parks, and this one is considered among the best.

Families tired of the rustic cabins found in many parks will be pleasantly surprised by the modern "lodge" that looks more like an expensive, state-of-the-art hotel. It was added in 1991. Accommodations include 120 guest rooms in the main hotel and 20 two- or four-bedroom furnished cottages (reserve well in advance), set in the park's wetlands and with screened-in porches and fireplaces. The park is run by Xanterra Parks and Resorts, which operates some of the country's best-known resorts.

And if bird-watching, bicycling, and sunsets over Lake Erie aren't enough to fill a visit, there's also an indoor and outdoor pool; beach; tennis; racquetball and basketball courts; restaurants and lounges; an exercise room and sauna; a nature center; a playground; an eighteen-hole Scottish-style golf course; and an amphitheater. Rates vary by room size and season.

Waterville

Garden Smiles (ages 5 and up)
211 Mechanic Street; (419) 878–5412; www.carruthstudio.com. Open from 10:00 A.M. to 6:00 P.M. Monday through Friday, 10:00 A.M. to 4:00 P.M. Saturday, and 12:30 to 4:30 P.M. Sunday. Free.

Hoping to raise a generation of green thumbs? This historic community, about ten minutes from Toledo, is home to one of America's best-known garden artists. Sculptor George Carruth displays his fun and whimsical work in this Maumee River town's historic downtown. Much of Carruth's inspiration comes from nature and from vintage children's books, making his work equally popular with young and old.

Garden Smiles, his gallery and shop, is the home of many unique designs that are handcast in stone. Among Carruth's many subjects are frogs, toads, hedgehogs, squirrels, and Mother Nature. Carruth's work appears in garden catalogs, galleries, and private collections, including the National Cathedral in Washington, D.C., and the ornament collection of the White House Christmas tree. Visitors from across the country travel to the store to buy Carruth pieces that are not available elsewhere and to have the artist sign his work. The shop also sells irregular pieces at a savings of 50 to 70 percent. A second store is located in Columbus's Polaris Towne Center (614–847–3660).

Port Clinton

African Safari Wildlife Park (ages 2 and up) 🐘
267 Lightner Road; (419) 732–3606, (800) 521–2660; www.africansafariwildlifepark .com. Open May through October. Ages seven and up $$$, children ages three to six $$, and free for those two and under.

Follow along the western shores of Lake Erie, and you'll soon reach African Wildlife Safari Park. Don your safari hats, but forget those scenes from *Jurassic Park*; the most dangerous encounters you're likely to have are with lovable llamas, amiable alpacas, and friendly zebras, all of which may wander around your family car or van as you drive through the one-hundred-acre enclave, the only drive-through safari park in the Midwest. More than 200 animals were born here in 2005, making the park one of the leaders in U.S. conservation efforts. Don't miss the warthogs—fewer than seventy-five still live in the United States—as well as the alpacas, white zebras, and rare giant elands. A bucket of food is included in the admission price, and the more aggressive animals come up to beg, leaving long, wet tongue marks on the side of your vehicle.

The park, open seasonally, boasts one of the largest alpaca and llama exhibits in the United States as well as two rare white zebras, two of only a few in the world and the only ones in the United States. More than 400 animals roam free among the park's grasslands.

Longing to get a little closer? Take a **free** ride on a pony or a camel, pet an ostrich, or feed the baby animals in Safari Junction. Burn off a little energy in the new Jungle Junction Playland, or fuel up at the Mobassa Cafe or one of the many picnic areas in Safari Junction. Afterward, check out the popular Porkchop Downs pig races and other types of amusing animal entertainment held daily during the summer.

Don't leave without casting a vote in the park's "Beauty or Beast" contest. A special exhibit featuring the rare African warthog (officially known as the tongue-twisting *Phacochoerus aethiopicus* but nicknamed "Buford") asks you to rate the looks of the warthog. The park calls him the world's ugliest animal, but others find his quirky looks appealing. You decide.

Where to Eat

Cisco and Charlie's Restaurant & Cantina, 1632 East Perry Street; (419) 732–3126. Known for its informal, border-style decor that's perfect for kids. Has a fun children's menu. $

Phil's Inn, 1704-8 East Perry Street; (419) 734–9023. A casual spot known for its "World Famous Spaghetti Sauce" and kids' menu. Rooms are also available. $–$$

Where to Stay

Best Western Port Clinton, 1734 East Perry Street; (419) 734–2274. Across from Lake Erie, with forty-one rooms and an on-site laundry, a boon for families. $

Fairfield Inn by Marriott, 3760 East State Road; (419) 732–2434. Sixty-four clean and comfortable rooms, some with water views. Rooms have free movies; there's also a complimentary breakfast bar and in-room Jacuzzi tub. $–$$

Holiday Inn Express Hotel & Suites, 50 Northeast Catawba Road; (419) 732–7322. New one-hundred-room hotel near ferries and Cedar Point. $–$$

For More Information

Port Clinton Area Chamber of Commerce, (419) 734–5503; www.portclintonchamber.com.

Lake Erie Islands (all ages)

It doesn't take long to reach the Lake Erie Islands. They're just a short ferryboat ride from Port Clinton or Sandusky, but you'll swear you've traveled much farther. There's an otherworldly feeling about this string of islands, which are 12 miles from Sandusky. The movie *Somewhere in Time* may have been filmed on Michigan's Mackinac Island, but it could easily have taken place here. A number of companies offer frequent ferry runs (hourly in summer) that transport you back and forth easily from the mainland to three of the five islands. Sightseeing tours are also a good way to take in the scenery, some of which was recently featured on the NBC *Today* show.

Lake Erie **Fishing**

Not surprisingly, Lake Erie fishing is a popular sport at Maumee Bay State Park and in other parts of northwest Ohio. Your amateur anglers will fall hook, line, and sinker for the tasty but testy walleye, which bite here from mid-May through mid-October. They're so numerous that Lake Erie's western basin is known as the Walleye Capital of the World, providing nearly two-thirds of the fish harvested from Ohio's Lake Erie waters each year.

The current state walleye record—15.95 pounds—was taken by a spring angler in 1995 off Sandusky Bay. The state smallmouth bass record—9.8 pounds—was taken off the Bass Islands. A license is required, of course.

While walleye and yellow perch are among the most popular catches for Lake Erie anglers, other common species include white bass, smallmouth bass, freshwater drum, channel catfish, and white perch. For the truly hardy, ice fishing is popular on the lake during January and February. Just be sure to remember the long underwear. For more information on Erie County fishing and numerous area charters, call (800) 255–ERIE (3743).

Kelleys Island

Each island has its own appeal, but Kelleys Island is the most remote and offers a great escape for the adventurous family or one seeking an easygoing vacation unspoiled by other people or cars. The largest American island on Lake Erie, the entire island is listed on the National Register of Historic Places. Once on the island, most visitors get to the pristine shoreline and the island's two popular archaeological sites by biking or driving golf carts (rentals are available).

Glacial Grooves State Memorial, on the island's north side, features smooth black limestone gullies carved some 30,000 years ago by Ice Age glaciers. This 400-foot-long stretch is considered one of the finest sets of glacial markings in the United States. Kelleys Island also boasts the fine Inscription Rock State Memorial, found on the south side. Prehistoric pictographs show various animal forms and human figures smoking pipes and wearing headdresses. They were carved by Native Americans from the Erie tribe, who were attracted here by the abundant fish in the area. (Walleye and perch are still island specialties; they can be had with hand-dipped onion rings at the popular Village Pump restaurant in the small village.)

Are your kids hiking fans? Acres of uninterrupted countryside, mostly preserved through state ownership, provide miles of trails. Lace up and head for the wooded North Shore Loop Trail. Cedar trees and milkweed, covered with monarch butterflies, blanket the East Quarry Trail, where even pint-size geologists will unearth fossils and other natural treasures.

Exploring **Davy Jones's Locker**

Trivia time: Did you know Ohio's waters are rich in shipwrecks? As the shallowest of the Great Lakes, Lake Erie has some 1,700 wrecks, including 50 off Kelleys Island. Grab your scuba or snorkel gear and head for Ohio's North Coast for some exciting underwater adventures. A set of guides to the wrecks is available from Ohio Sea Grant at www.sg.ohio-state.edu. It also has information about dive tours if you don't want to go it alone.

Where to Eat

Village Pump, 103 West Lakeshore Drive, Kelleys Island; (419) 746–2281. A friendly pub-style eatery known for its Lake Erie perch and walleye as well as stacked sandwiches. $

Water St. Cafe, Lakeshore and Division Streets, Kelleys Island; (419) 746–2468. Open year-round (an island rarity), this casual restaurant is known for pizza, perch, burgers, and its extensive kids' menu. $–$$

Where to Stay

Eagles Nest B&B, P.O. Box 762, Kelleys Island 43456; (419) 625–9635. Four rooms, continental breakfast; children welcome. You'll stay in your own cozy suite surrounded by scenic woods. $

Kelleys Island State Park, Kelleys Island; (419) 797–4530. One hundred twenty-nine sites perfect for family-size tents, as well as convenient showers. Pets are permitted, in case you decide to bring Fido along for the ride. $

For More Information

Kelleys Island Chamber of Commerce, 130 Division Street, Kelleys Island 43438; (419) 746–2360; www.kelleysisland.com.

South Bass Island/Put-in-Bay

If you and your kids like a little more man-made excitement, consider a stay at Put-in-Bay, the bustling port on South Bass Island. You'll find wildlife of another kind on this island, which was named for its sheltered harbor that protected sailors during stormy weather. It's been sheltering families looking for sun and fun ever since.

Good ways to see the island include by bicycle (rentals available near the docks), kayak (available near Oak Pointe State Park), and parasail (register at the boardwalk).

Amazing Ohio Facts

South Bass Island's Heineman Winery is home to Crystal Cave, the world's only walk-in geode, where celestite crystals dangle from the walls like diamond earrings.

Perry's Victory and Peace Monument (ages 2 and up)
Open daily 10:00 A.M. to 7:00 P.M. mid-June through Labor Day, 10:00 A.M. to 5:00 P.M. late April through mid-June; www.put-in-bay.com/perry. Elevator ride to top for adults $, free for children sixteen and under.

Here you can climb the steps and take in the great view 352 feet above water from the Perry's Victory and Peace Monument (there's also an elevator for the unadventurous). The monument was named for Comm. Oliver Perry, who sought refuge on the island during the War of 1812. Its observation deck offers breathtaking views of the neighboring islands and Lake Erie's blue expanse. New in 2002, the $2.4 million visitor center features a movie about the War of 1812, historical displays, and an 1860 statue of Perry on loan from the city of Perrysburg, Ohio.

Kimberley's Carousel (all ages)
On Delaware Avenue. Open May through October. $

While downtown, don't miss a spin on one of the few remaining merry-go-rounds with all wooden horses in the United States. This Allen Herschell machine was built in New York State in 1917. Its crown is decorated with hand-painted panels depicting famous island landmarks.

Perry's Cave (ages 3 and up)
(419) 285–2405. Open daily in summer from 10:30 A.M. to 6:00 P.M. $

Commodore Perry is also the namesake and the 1813 discoverer of Perry's Cave, where spelunkers can take twenty-minute tours more than 50 feet below the surface of South Bass Island. Tradition has it that Perry stored supplies and kept prisoners in the cave during the battle of Lake Erie.

Just 0.5 mile from downtown, the cave is 208 feet long by 165 feet wide. It was first shown to the public in 1870 for the grand fee of 10 cents per person. (Today it's slightly more.) The walls, ceiling, and cave floor are covered with calcium carbonate, which settled from centuries of dripping water; an underground lake, where the water level rises and falls with Lake Erie, is located inside as well. At one time the island's Victory Hotel, once the largest in the world, pumped its water from the cave's lake.

Today visitors can still see the ruins of that hotel, which burned in 1919, in South Bass Island State Park. The cave also offers spooky lantern tours, a shaded picnic area, and the Shop on the Top, where kids can mine for gems or pick up a memento of their adventure. An eighteen-hole minigolf course with a War of 1812 theme and a rock climbing wall were added in 2002.

Crystal Cave (ages 3 and up)

(419) 285–2811. Admission to the cave is included in the tour of the island's Heineman Winery on Catawba Avenue. Tours, including juice or wine, $.

Put-in-Bay is also home to Crystal Cave, which workers found in 1897 while digging a well on the island. After some exploration, they realized that the 40-foot pocket they had dug was part of a geode (hollow pockets that are lined with beautiful sparkling crystals).

Today Crystal Cave is known as the world's largest geode. Samples of the largest celestite crystals found here are now part of an exhibition at the Smithsonian Institution in Washington, D.C.

For More Information

Put-in-Bay Chamber of Commerce, P.O. Box 250, Put-in-Bay 43456; (419) 285–2832; www.put-in-bay.com.

Middle Bass Island

The fishing on Middle Bass Island has been attracting anglers—including Presidents Harrison and Cleveland—for years. Once called Isle de Fleurs, or flower island, by missionaries who visited in 1680, Middle Bass and its neighbors North and Small Bass are named, not surprisingly, for the abundant smallmouth bass swimming in these waters. Middle Bass is a serene island of great natural beauty. Parts of the island are being developed as a new state park. The state purchased more than 120 acres on the 758-acre island's southern tip; watch for developments.

Where to Eat

The Boardwalk, on the waterfront. Serves seafood, pizza, burgers, and a legendary lobster bisque. $–$$

Brewery at the Bay, 441 Catawba Avenue, Put-in-Bay; (419) 285–HOPS. Pizza, sandwiches, and microbrews attract a diverse crowd. Live entertainment on weekends. $–$$

Where to Stay

Bay Lodging House, 405 Lakeview Avenue, Put-in-Bay; (419) 285–2041. Has both hotel rooms and two-bedroom units with kitchens perfect for families. $–$$

For More Information

Erie County Visitors Bureau, (800) 255–3743; www.buckeyenorth.com.

Ottawa County Visitors Bureau, (800) 441–1271; www.lake-erie.com.

Lakeside

Looking for a little peace and quiet on your next vacation? Back on the mainland, look no further than Lakeside, the idyllic community known as "Chatauqua on Lake Erie." Families have been coming to this historic Victorian community on the Marblehead Peninsula, east of Port Clinton, since the turn of the twentieth century. The community celebrated its 125th anniversary in 1999.

Religious leaders once gathered here for spiritual retreat and rebirth. As more and more families joined them, Lakeside became increasingly known as a family vacation paradise. Today, although religious life is still an important part of the Lakeside season, the emphasis is on fellowship, personal growth, and arts appreciation. Day visitors can pick up a daily pass that entitles them to enjoy activities that range from

Author on the Lam in Lakeside

I've traveled all around the world on travel-writing assignments, but I have to admit I've never been busted until a trip to Lakeside, Ohio. Actually, busted is a bit of an overstatement—reprimanded is a little more like it.

I had taken advantage of a beautiful summer morning by lacing up my in-line skates and exploring the gated enclave's Victorian-style cottages, scenic Lake Erie shoreline, and charming vintage downtown. It was still early, and my family was sleeping back at the hotel. Few people were about, except for some elderly residents who gave me strange looks as I skated past. Shrugging it off, I continued on my tour.

A few minutes later, a squad car slowed down and pulled me over. "Excuse me, miss, but we don't allow in-line skating in the downtown district," he said politely. "Some older people are worried about safety," he explained, "and we like to keep our downtown as authentic as we can." What? They didn't have in-line skates at the turn of the twentieth century?

the Lakeside Symphony, ballet companies, lectures, and choral events to freewheeling children's programs. At any given time during the summer season, the grounds and the huge 700-foot dock are alive with families swimming, sailing, fishing, strolling, or simply enjoying another beautiful day on the water.

Where to Stay

Hotel Lakeside, 236 Walnut Avenue; (419) 798–4461. This grand, one-hundred-room hotel has great views of Lake Erie from its wide porch and vintage-style rooms that are a favorite with area families. The dining room serves up old-fashioned entrees, including a popular Friday fish fry. $–$$

For More Information

The Lakeside Association, (419) 798–4461; www.lakesideohio.com.

Marblehead

Not far from Lakeside, the oldest operating lighthouse on the Great Lakes attracts lighthouse enthusiasts of all ages.

Marblehead Lighthouse State Park (all ages) 🏛

Tours are offered weekday afternoons from 1:00 to 4:45 P.M. May through August and on the second Saturday of the month June through October. For information contact the Peninsula Chamber of Commerce, P.O. Box 268, Marblehead 43440; (419) 798–9777, (419) 797–4530; www.dnr.state.oh.us/parks/marblehead. Free.

The Marblehead Lighthouse is one of the most scenic lighthouses in the state and a great spot for a family photo. Built in 1821, this 85-foot-tall limestone light was constructed in just eleven weeks. The first keeper, Benajah Wolcott, kept the thirteen lamps fueled with whale oil; later the whale oil was replaced by a Fresnel lens, imported from France in 1903, which reflects light through refraction. Updated with electricity in 1923, the lighthouse retired its lens in 1969. Today the lighthouse's new 300 mm light flashes a green glow every three seconds. The area around the lighthouse is also the home of a small artists' community located at the peninsula's tip and the busiest U.S. Coast Guard station on the Great Lakes.

Johnson Island

Only a few hundred yards down Bayshore Road, a historic marker identifies the causeway leading to Johnson Island, with its famous Civil War Confederate Prison Camp. Originally named Bull's Island (prisoners referred to the prison as the Bull Pen), the island's 330 acres on Sandusky Bay were home to some 9,000 Confederate officers, Union defectors, and civilians between 1862 and 1865. Of the original 9,000 prisoners, some 206 remain on the island, memorialized in white marble in the island's cemetery. It's a fascinating—if sobering—piece of Ohio history, one that makes quite an impression on older kids.

Sandusky

Although Sandusky is a pretty Victorian town, few families take the time to discover it. Most are too intent on reaching the city's star attraction—Cedar Point. It's worth slowing down and wandering through the historic town after your Cedar Point stay, however, if you want to discover some of the area's other, lower key, old-fashioned charms.

Cedar Point (ages 1 and up) 🎢 🐘 🎵 🏛️

Located off U.S. Highway 6, ten minutes north of Ohio Turnpike; (419) 627–2106; www.cedarpoint.com. Hours and admission vary with season. Adults and kids over 48 inches tall $$$$, kids under 48 inches tall and seniors $$, free for kids under two.

When I was a kid, summer began the day my family went to Cedar Point. My sister and I looked forward to it each year. As school drew to a close, we'd start badgering our parents about our annual trek to the amusement park, and we didn't let up till we were in the car and heading east.

Almost thirty years later, Cedar Point remains one of Ohio's top family destinations. And much of what draws them is what drew us all those years ago: roller coasters (the most in the world), snow cones, sun, and fun.

Now more than 130 years old, Cedar Point has changed since the days when its biggest attraction was a dance hall. Today it is best known for its many scream machines (including the 205-foot-tall Magnum XL–200; the soaring Raptor; the Mean Streak; the wicked, thirteen-story Demon Drop; the Tower of Power; and the newest, Top Thrill Dragster, the tallest and fastest coaster in the world, added in 2003—the only roller coaster in the world to break the 400-foot-tall milestone) and sixty more down-to-earth rides spread out over 364 acres.

But there are alternatives to being spun, twisted, dropped, or turned upside down. Check out the IMAX film at the cinema. Come nose to nose with performing sea creatures at Oceana Stadium. Wander the Lake Erie beach and boardwalk. Dance along to live stage shows. Get away from it all on the cable cars or space spiral.

Little ones have their own pint-size fun, with seventeen miniature rides in Kiddy Kingdom, including a small-scale roller coaster, bumper boats, and a drive-it-yourself four-by-four truck that looks just like the grown-up model. There's barnyard fun at the petting farm and the popular Berenstein Bear Country, with tree houses, ball crawls, and other playground favorites. Camp Snoopy was added in 1999, as well as roaming *Peanuts* characters. In 2000 *Thrill Ride* magazine named Cedar Point "favorite amusement/theme park."

And if all that wasn't enough, there's Challenge Park and the new-and-improved Soak City Water Park, which recently doubled in size, with three new rides, including a gigantic, high-action water slide featuring six-person rafts; an inner-tube river adventure; and two playground areas (both parks have separate admission charges). My kids confess to liking Soak City almost as much as the park itself.

Formerly a Cedar Point hotel, the new indoor Castaway Bay water park opened in 2004, partly in an effort to compete with the wildly successful and nearby Great Wolf Lodge, also in Sandusky. It features 38,000 square feet of fun that's all wet. The tropical Caribbean theme extends to the enclosed five-story waterpark, featuring a vaulted wood ceiling, palm trees, lazy lagoons, and more.

New in 2001 was Lighthouse Point, a cabin/cottage area of accommodations behind the Mean Streak roller coaster. It's a great place to stay—and the view of Lake Erie is spectacular.

Surviving **Cedar Point**

Sure, it's no Disney World, but on a summer day Cedar Point can look like downtown Calcutta. After annual trips as a child and now with my own two children, I consider myself a veteran. As such, I've come up with a few survival tips to make the trip easier on parents. Remember, it's all about having fun!

- Buy your tickets ahead of time so you don't have to wait in line. Many organizations offer discounted tickets if you buy them in advance, and you won't have to wait in the long entry lines.

- Consider packing a cooler from home. Cuisine choices in the park are limited and can blow the budget. (Don't miss the french fries by the aquarium, however, and be sure to sprinkle them with vinegar for a true taste treat.) You can pack sandwiches and snacks and leave them on a picnic table in the area by the admission gate. No one will bother them, and you can wander back whenever you need a break.

- If all else fails and you truly need a break, take the kids to the park's Soak City area, where they can splash and play while you take turns enjoying the swim-up bar. Who says you're not in the Caribbean?

Erie Island **Cruises (all ages)**

Sandusky is also home base for day cruises in and around the Lake Erie Islands. For the first-time visitor, this is the perfect way to get a handle on what the area holds and where you'd like to come back to next time. Many packages offer meals as part of the deal.

Looking for a good time? Look no further than the *Goodtime I*, the last of the cruise companies offering regular island-hopping service. It's at Jackson Street Pier and offers daily tours to Kelleys Island and Put-in-Bay. The *Goodtime I* is a 365-passenger boat with full bar service, dance floor, and snack bar. Adults $$$$, children ages four to twelve $$$. Call (800) 446–3140.

Merry-Go-Round Museum (ages 2 to 7)

30 Jackson Street; (419) 626–6111; www.merrygoroundmuseum.org. Open year-round; weekends only in January and February. $, free for kids under four.

Merry-go-rounds may seem a trifle tame after a day at Cedar Point, but they have a certain nostalgic charm that's perennially appealing, especially to toddlers and younger children who may be a little overwhelmed by Cedar Point's frantic pace. Relive the glory days of the carousel and other classic Americana with a tour of the Merry-Go-Round Museum, housed in the city's former 1920s downtown post office. The museum was recently awarded a grant from the National Endowment for the Humanities to preserve the National Carousel Archives.

Highlights include the working Allen Herschell carousel from the 1930s (a free ride is part of the tour) and the original Gustav Dentzel carving shop from Philadelphia. Frequent exhibitions and speakers feature carousel history; classes and concerts are offered. There's also a small English carousel from the beginning of the twentieth century; a gift shop stocked with virtually every carousel-related item known to man; traveling exhibitions; and a full-time, on-premises carver/restorer.

Toft's Dairy (all ages)

3717 Venice Road, on the city's outskirts; (419) 625–4376, (800) 521–4606; www.toft dairy.com.

After a relaxing visit to Sandusky, be sure to stop to get in a lick or two at Toft's Dairy near the edge of town. This local dairy has been serving up creamy confections since 1900, when it was founded as a small farm with a respected herd of dairy cattle. In 1935 it acquired another retail dairy, the beginnings of the modern operation. Since then the dairy has moved three times, and it now services towns as far as Michigan and outlying parts of Ohio. It is the only locally owned and operated dairy on Lake Erie between Lorain and Toledo. Parlors are also located in Fremont and Port Clinton; check the Web site for directions.

Tours are offered daily. Afterward, sample classic flavors such as butter pecan and vanilla or the newer favorites, such as Moose Tracks and Mother Lode, full of chocolate and caramel. Kids often opt for the chewy Dinosaur Crunch.

Lagoon Deer Park (all ages)

Off Highway 269; (419) 684–5701. Open mid-April through mid-October. Hours and prices vary with season.

Sandusky is also home to Lagoon Deer Park, where you and your kids can get up close and personal with more than 250 animals from Europe, Japan, Asia, South and North America, and other worldwide locations. Hand-feed hundreds of deer and other tame species, feed fish, or cast your pole in stocked lagoons and fishing lakes. If you visit in spring, look for the park's newest additions—seventy-five baby animals are born here each year. Don't miss the famous Dancing Chicken. The grounds also have attractive picnic facilities and a gift shop.

Great Wolf Lodge (all ages)

4600 Milan Road; (888) 779–2327, (419) 609–6000; www.greatwolflodge.com.

More (much more) than just a place to stay, the new Great Wolf is the next best thing to Cedar Point—especially in winter (in summer you can combine the two). This hot new attraction opened in 2001 as Ohio's first indoor waterpark and features 33,000 square feet of fun. The five-story indoor park includes body slides, tube rides, quiet pools, water cannons, and 271 family suites, where you can recover at night before getting up and doing it all again. Room rates include four waterpark passes (extras are $15 each). A two-night minimum stay is required.

Kalahari Lodge (all ages)

7000 Kalahari Drive; (877) 525–2427; www.kalahariresorts.com. $$$

Travel from the Alaskan wilderness to the African continent without leaving Ohio. With three indoor waterparks to choose from, Ohio offers a range of choices. The Kalahari Lodge is the newest and, some say, one of the most exciting. With the Swahili Swirl, 400-foot-long tube slide, the Victoria Falls raft slide, and more, it's the largest too.

Where to Eat

DeMore's Fish Den, 302 West Perkins; (419) 626–8861. Home of the "Giant Perch Sandwich," DeMore's is known for its great prices and casual dining on an outdoor patio. Specialties include perch and walleye. $

Perkins Family Restaurant, 1530 Cleveland Road; (419) 625–9234. A reliable, comfortable family favorite with a varied menu. $

Where to Stay

There are plenty of places to stay near Cedar Point. If you want to forgo the cost (and convenience) of staying inside the park's gates, consider the following choices. All are pretty basic, but after a day at the park you'll probably just be looking for a place to sleep.

Best Western Cedar Point, U.S. Highway 6, 1530 Cleveland Road; (419) 625–9234. Conveniently located, the chain is known for reliable service and spacious rooms that cater to families. The adjacent Perkins Restaurant is a good, basic place to eat, with a range of kid-pleasing entrees. $

Fairfield Inn by Marriott, 6220 Milan Road; (419) 621–9500. A good budget bet that includes a continental breakfast (a good thing if you have hungry adolescents!) and a comfortable room. $

Radisson Harbour Inn, 2001 Cleveland Road; (419) 627–2500. A bit pricey, but large, convenient, and just minutes from the park gate. Owned by Cedar Point. $$

For More Information

Sandusky/Erie County Visitors Bureau, (800) 255–3743; www.buckeye north.com.

Milan

Thomas Edison's Birthplace/Milan Historical Museum
(ages 5 and up)
9 North Edison Drive; (419) 499–2135 for the birthplace; (419) 499–2968 for the museum; www.tomedison.org or www.milanohio.com. **Hours vary with attraction and season. $$; under six free.**

About 13 miles south of Sandusky is Thomas Edison's Birthplace. This simple, seven-room, two-and-one-half-story home built in 1841 housed the famous inventor of the phonograph and the lightbulb from the time he was born in 1847 until he was seven years old, when the family moved to Port Huron, Michigan. The museum was opened by Edison's daughter on February 11, 1947—the day he would have turned one hundred.

Today it is run by his great-grandson and furnished with many original family pieces. Don't miss the room honoring his many inventions, including phonographs, lightbulbs, and models of his movie studio and Menlo Park laboratory. Other examples of Edisonia include examples of his early inventions, documents, and family mementos. (Edison held 1,093 American patents.)

The adjacent Milan Historical Museum houses the respected Coulton Doll Collection, with more than 360 rare dolls from many periods and the Moury Glass collection. It also features a blacksmith's shop and a vintage general store. The museum is closed in December and January.

Bellevue

Seneca Caverns (ages 4 and up)

15248 East Thompson Road; (419) 483–6711; www.senecacavernsohio.com. Open Memorial Day through Labor Day and weekends in May, September, and through mid-October. Adults $$, children ages five to twelve $, under five free.

Southeast of Milan is Bellevue, where you can "go underground" during a visit to Seneca Caverns, located south of the city. This 110-foot-deep cave—technically an "earth crack"—was discovered in 1872 by two boys hunting rabbits, when their dog fell into what they thought was a sinkhole.

The cavern opened to the public in 1933. Today visitors descend steps 110 feet underground through seven levels to an underground river on hour-long tours that are offered from May 1 through October 15. The largest room is 250 feet in length. Be sure to bring a sweater—the temperature never rises above fifty-four degrees.

The cavern is fairly rugged—a fact kids love—and it is one of the few in the country kept in its original natural condition. Don't leave without panning for gems at the Seneca/Ole Mist'ry River Gem Mining or enjoying a picnic in the shade.

Historic Lyme Village (ages 4 and up)

5001 Highway 4; (419) 483–4949; www.lymevillage.com. Open Tuesday to Sunday from 1:00 to 5:00 P.M. Adults $$, children ages six to twelve $.

Bellevue is also home to historic Lyme Village, a tribute to a local farmer named John Wright, who did well and went on to build an impressive Victorian mansion complete with a third-floor ballroom. Today that mansion is joined by fifteen other buildings that re-create an Ohio village, Victorian-style. Besides the residence there are three log houses, a schoolhouse, a farm, a general store, a hardware store, a post office, and more. Daily demonstrations of spinning, weaving, blacksmithing, and candle making offer children a fascinating glimpse of a bygone way of life.

Ohio **Celebrities**

Thomas Edison may be one of the state's most famous native sons, but he's certainly not the only one. Other illustrious one-time Ohioans include naturalist John James Audubon; U.S. Army officer George Custer; lawyer Clarence Darrow; songwriter Stephen Foster; baseball player Cy Young; inventors Orville and Wilbur Wright; astronauts John Glenn, James Lovell Jr., and Neil Armstrong; actors Clark Gable and Bob Hope; and Wild West star Annie Oakley.

For More Information

Bellevue Area Tourism and Visitors Bureau, (800) 562–6978; www.bellevue tourism.org.

Tiffin

Crystal Traditions Tours (ages 6 and up)

145 Madison Street; (419) 448–4286, (888) 298–7236; www.crystaltraditions.com.
Showroom and outlet open Monday to Friday 10:00 A.M. to 5:00 P.M. and Saturday
10:00 A.M. to 2:00 P.M. Free.

Maxwell Crystal, on Madison Street, gives tours throughout the day and celebrates
the area's glass industry, which dates to the late nineteenth century. Wander through
the company's production facilities on one of three free guided tours, and you'll
watch Maxwell's signature glassblowing and glass-engraving employees at work.
There's a gift shop on the premises and an outlet if you'd like to pick up a few goodies
to take home.

Seneca County Museum (ages 6 and up)

28 Clay Street; (419) 447–5955. Hours vary. Free.

Show your kids the finished product at the Seneca County Museum, which displays a
rare and extensive grouping of Tiffin glass in a well-preserved historic house (circa
1853). Examples also can be seen at the Glass Heritage Gallery (419–435–5077),
which is about 14 miles away in nearby Fostoria. Examples include lamps, crystal
bowls, art glass, and more.

Where to Eat

Pioneer Mill, 255 Riverside Drive; (419)
448–8662. Offers relaxing dining for parents and a pleasing kids' menu in a historic
1822 structure. $–$$

Where to Stay

Quality Inn, 1927 South Highway 53;
(419) 447–6313. Seventy-three rooms; on-
site restaurant, cable TV, and a laundry. $

Mansfield

Richland Carrousel Park (all ages)

75 North Main Street; (419) 522–4223; www.richlandcarrousel.com. Open 10:00 A.M. to 5:00 P.M. daily in summer, otherwise 11:00 A.M. to 5:00 P.M. $

On summer days, the sounds of Richland's restored band organ waft through the streets, setting a festive mood. Take a ride on the 1930s hand-carved carousel. Afterward, try the 1991 version, the first built in the United States since the 1930s. You can wander through the surrounding restored area, which includes gift shops, a bookstore, and snack stops offering ice cream, coffee, and a bite to eat.

Living Bible Museum (all ages)

500 Tingley Avenue; (419) 524–0139, (800) 222–0139; www.livingbiblemuseum.org. Open April through December Monday through Friday from 10:00 A.M. to 5:00 P.M., Saturday from 10:00 A.M. to 7:00 P.M., Sunday 2:00 to 7:00 P.M. year-round. $; children under age six **free.**

Two family-focused museums provide more than fifty life-size inspirational dioramas on the life of Christ and the miracles of the Old Testament as well as special effects, Ohio's only wax museum, and more. A collection of rare Bibles, immigrant American religious folk art, and various woodcarvings are also featured.

Where to Eat

Troyers Dutch Heritage, 720 Highway 97 West, Bellville; (419) 886–7070. Home-cooked Amish-style cooking, bakery, and on-site minigolf.

Bucyrus

Bucyrus Bratwurst Festival (all ages)

301 South Sandusky Avenue; (419) 562–2728.

What would summer be without cooking more than twenty-seven tons of bratwurst for a few thousand of your closest friends? The ultimate backyard cookout takes place in the "Bratwurst Capital of America" for three days in August. Besides offering more than one hundred stands that serve up a variety of dogs and brats, the festival has rides, games, daily parades, craft booths, and plenty of **free** entertainment.

Southern Northwest Ohio

While northwest Ohio is known far and wide for its lakeshore, the southern part of the region offers many family attractions as well. Zip south along Interstate 75 and you'll pass a number of spots well worth a stop.

Bowling Green

You can't miss Bowling Green. The signs for Bowling Green State University are the first clue that you're getting close, followed by the huge football stadium. The university dominates the town and is known for its attractive, 1,300-acre campus surrounded by fertile farmland.

Educational Memorabilia Center (ages 5 and up) 🏛 🔖

Bowling Green State University; (419) 372–2531; www.bgsu.edu. Hours limited; the center is closed when the university is not in session. Free.

It's not surprising to find the Educational Memorabilia Center in this learning-oriented town. The red, one-room schoolhouse from 1875 was moved from Norwalk, Ohio, 60 miles to the east, and rebuilt in 1975 in time for the country's bicentennial.

After a visit, your kids may never gripe about going to school again. The schoolhouse is decorated with furnishings typical of the era: potbellied stove, fabric blackboard, uncomfortable wooden desks. Two doors mark the entrance—one for boys, one for girls. Display cases house memorabilia such as the center's collection of rare McGuffey reading charts, a century-old ketchup bottle that was found when the building was dismantled, and even a tombstone that formed the original school sign (tour guides speculate that it was an early attempt at recycling). On-premises tour guides give twenty-minute lectures about school life at the time.

National Tractor Pulling Championship (ages 5 and up)

P.O. Box 401, Wood County Fairgrounds 43402; (419) 354–1434; www.ntpapull.com. $$$; free for children ages ten and under.

Bowling Green is also home to the National Tractor Pulling Championship, the world's largest outdoor tractor pull. Now in its fortieth year, it's held each year in late August at the Wood County Fairgrounds. The event is especially popular with preschool and early school-age boys.

Mary Jane Thurston State Park (all ages) 🛶 🎿

Interstate 466, Highway 65, McClure; (419) 832–7662; www.dnr.state.oh.us/parks. Open dawn to dusk. Free.

If you visit in winter, make snowshoe tracks to Mary Jane Thurston State Park near Napoleon. This 591-acre park has fishing, boating, and hiking in summer but is renowned in the area for its exciting downhill sledding.

Where to Eat

Fricker's, 1720 East Wooster; (419) 354–2000. Casual and fun sports-bar decor and a menu of kid-friendly favorites make this a good bet. $

Where to Stay

Best Western Falcon Plaza Motel, 1450 East Wooster; (419) 352–4671, (800) 528–1234. A handy location opposite the college and free movies make this a popular spot. $$

Quality Inn and Suites, 1630 East Wooster; (419) 352–2521, (800) 4–CHOICE. Spacious rooms (many are suites), an on-site restaurant, and a pool attract families to this well-run hostelry across from Bowling Green State University. $$

For More Information

Bowling Green Convention and Visitors Bureau, (800) 866–0046; www.visit bgohio.org.

Lima

Venture a little farther south along Interstate 75 and you'll hit Lima. This small city, nicknamed "Ohio's Hometown," is known for its 1933 connection to gangster John Dillinger. After Dillinger's gang killed the town sheriff, the shooting led to a nation-wide manhunt. It is also home to the U.S. Plastics Corporation, one of the area's largest employers.

U.S. Plastics Corporation (ages 7 and up)
1390 Neubrecht Road; (419) 228–2242. Call ahead for tour information. Free.

Visitors can get an up-close view of the rotational mold process used in producing industrial plastic containers during a guided walking tour and instructional video and then take advantage of discounts on more than 13,000 plastic home, office, and garden products in the outlet store.

Allen County Museum (ages 5 and up)
620 West Market Street; (419) 222–9426; www.allencountymuseum.org. Open Tuesday through Saturday 1:00 to 5:00 P.M. Free.

You'll find a little bit of everything at this small but special museum, including Native American and pioneer items, railroad memorabilia, antique cars and bikes, even a country store, doctor's office, and barbershop. Don't miss the 10- by 15-foot decorated model of Mount Vernon, the full-service locomotive, a log house, and the hands-on displaysfor kids, inlcuding a cool display of steam locomotives and an HO gauge model railroad.

Where to Eat

Bandido's Restaurante Mexicano,
2613 Elida Road; (419) 331–0855. This
casual-style cantina opposite Lima Mall features kid-friendly tacos, chips, and more,
and a popular Sunday brunch. $

Old Barn Out Back Restaurant, 3175
West Elm Street; (419) 991–3075. A local
family-style favorite. Try the lunch buffet
(choose from old-fashioned baked ham,
fried chicken, or country roast beef) and
go back for seconds (or thirds) at the all-
you-can-eat soup/salad/bread/dessert bar.
Take along a few of their famous rolls
topped with cinnamon butter for the road;
better yet, go back for breakfast. $

Where to Stay

Fairfield Inn, 2179 Elida Road; (419)
224–8496. Reliable, high-quality, budget
chain near shopping and restaurants.
Sixty-four rooms, **free** breakfast, heated
pool, and game room. $

Holiday Inn, 1816 Harding Highway;
(419) 222–0004. A family favorite, with a
pool (a must!) and on-site restaurant. Centrally located. $–$$

Wapakoneta

Wapakoneta has one main claim to fame: It put the first person on the moon. On July
20, 1969, one tiny step for Neil Armstrong became a giant leap for humankind when
he forever changed the face of American space exploration. Enthusiasts and sci-fi
buffs won't want to miss the white-domed Neil Armstrong Air and Space Museum,
which honors Armstrong and others who have contributed to human exploration of
space and sky.

Neil Armstrong Air & Space Museum (ages 4 and up) 🧑‍🦽

**Interstate 75, exit 111; (419) 738–8811, (800) 860–0142; www.ohiohistory.org. Open
Tuesday through Saturday from 9:30 A.M. to 5:00 P.M. and Sunday from noon to 5:00
P.M. Adults $$, children six to twelve $, under six free.**

Drivers on I-75 can't help but notice the museum's stark white dome from the free-
way. Opened in 1972, it reflects the boldness of man's venture in its unusual archi-
tecture. Earth is mounded around the frame of the building; a 56-foot dome covers
the theater.

A stop here reveals everything your amateur astronauts ever wanted to know
about humankind's venture into air and space. Seven galleries are filled with vintage
aircraft and spacecraft exhibits as well as artifacts such as moon rocks, model air-
plane collections, Armstrong's spacesuit, and samples of space food. A cubic room
of mirrors simulates the vastness of space.

Other must-see highlights include the *Toledo II,* the first manned and powered airship to grace the New York City skies; the *Gemini VIII* spacecraft flown by Armstrong in 1966; a model of the *Saturn V* rocket; and the Astro-Theater, which features a multimedia presentation of the sights and sounds of space against a starry sky. The annual Festival of Flight, held in mid-July, includes a model-rocket launch, a ham radio demonstration, airplane shows, food, and games.

Where to Stay and Eat

Best Western Wapakoneta, 1510 Saturn Road; (419) 738–8181. A handy spot next to the Armstrong Space Museum, **free** breakfast, and ninety-six spacious rooms make this a favorite with families. $-$$

Chalet Restaurant (419–738–6414), adjacent to the hotel, is open daily from 6:00 A.M. to 10:00 P.M. and has a great kids' menu as well as a fun, Bavarian atmosphere. $

Northeast Ohio

Northeast Ohio has an eclectic flavor all its own, from sleepy fishing villages reminiscent of America's East Coast and relaxing Lake Erie getaways to bustling big cities and major-league excitement. With the 1986 opening of the Cleveland Rock and Roll Hall of Fame and Museum, this region proved that it could really shake, rattle, and roll. And, if that weren't enough, your family can take in the World's Largest Tooth in Cleveland, rub noses with marine mammals at Six Flags in Aurora, tackle history at the Pro Football Hall of Fame in Canton, or hitch a ride on a horse-drawn buggy through Amish Country. It's all here waiting for you.

Khristi's TopPicks for fun in Northeast Ohio

1. Going nose to nose with dolphins at Six Flags (formerly Sea World)

2. Jammin' at the Rock and Roll Hall of Fame in Cleveland

3. Taking a horse-drawn carriage ride in Amish Country

4. Taking a trolley tour of Cleveland

5. Sleeping in a former grain silo in Akron

NORTHEAST OHIO

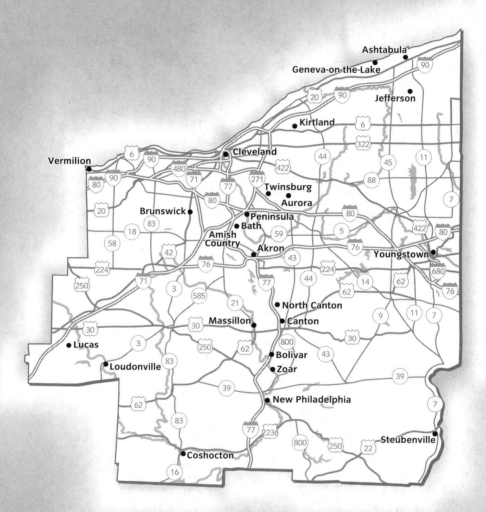

Ashtabula
Geneva-on-the-Lake
Jefferson
90
20
90
Kirtland
6
322
Vermilion
Cleveland
44
45
11
6
90
480
422
88
80
90
71
77
271
7
20
80
Twinsburg
Brunswick
80
Aurora
83
Peninsula
59
5
80
18
Bath
422
58
Amish
Country
42
Akron
76
43
Youngstown
224
Akron
44
224
62
680
250
71
3
585
21
77
62
14
76
North Canton
9
11
7
30
Lucas
3
30
Massillon
Canton
11
7
250
62
800
30
83
Bolivar
43
39
Loudonville
62
Zoar
39
39
83
New Philadelphia
7
77
2236
16
800
250
22
Steubenville
Coshocton
16

Vermilion

Inland Seas Maritime Museum (ages 3 and up) 🦀

480 Main Street; (800) 893–1485, (440) 967–3467; www.inlandseas.org. Open daily from 10:00 A.M. to 5:00 P.M. $

Tiny sailors can grab a steamer's helm or explore an authentic pilothouse as they imagine themselves navigating the mighty Great Lakes at the Inland Seas Maritime Museum. This charming lakeside town—one of the first you encounter as you skirt Lake Erie and enter northeast Ohio—is home to one of the few museums that celebrates life on the historic waterways known as the Great Lakes. Both levels were redesigned recently, giving the museum a spiffy new look. Plans were also announced to replace the existing facility with a new maritime museum on the Black River. The 40,000-square-foot facility will replace the current museum and include docking space for tall ships and other touring maritime attractions.

Pore over shipwright models, newspapers, photographs, and artifacts that capture the golden age of Great Lakes maritime history. Wander among vintage photographs, instruments, hands-on tools, and displays that tell the history of the Battle of Lake Erie. There are also timbers from the *Niagara* (Admiral Perry's 1812 flagship), a video that recounts the wreck of the *Edmund Fitzgerald*, and a well-stocked gift shop with books and mementos of Great Lakes life. Don't miss the 1877 lighthouse and the 1905 pilothouse.

Vermilion Lighthouse (all ages) 🏛

(440) 967–3467 or (800) 893–1485. Open daily from 10:00 A.M. to 5:00 P.M. Admission included in museum rate.

Adjacent to the Inland Seas Maritime Museum is the classic Vermilion Lighthouse, built in 1847, rebuilt in 1859, and finished in 1877. A 400-foot catwalk runs parallel to a concrete pier, linking the lighthouse to the mainland. The brave keeper used this walkway to reach the light whenever waves crested over the pier. When the lighthouse began tilting toward the busy harbor in 1929, it was dismantled by a group of concerned citizens. In 1992 it was rebuilt yet again. Today its rare 1891 Fresnel lens serves as a nighttime messenger once more.

For the **Birds**

North America's largest concentration of ring-billed gulls visits Lake Erie's western basin each fall. Other winged visitors include Bonaparte's great black-backed gulls and little, glaucous, and laughing gulls. For a free birding guide, call (800) 255–ERIE, and be sure to look up!

Where to Eat

Edna Mae's, 5598 Liberty Avenue; (440) 967–7733. A great old-fashioned ice-cream parlor sure to please sweet tooths of all ages. They also serve sandwiches and soups. $

Sal & Al's Diner, 2261 Cooper Foster Park Road, Amherst; (440) 282–4367. Don't leave the area without sampling the filling fare at Sal & Al's Diner. You'll be movin' and groovin' to the beat of an old-style jukebox as you feast on a menu loaded with 1950s favorites—all made from scratch—such as hot roast beef with mashed potatoes and gravy, barbecued pork sandwich, burgers 'n' fries, and BLTs.

Afterward, get a lick in at George's Tin Roof ice-cream parlor, which is next door. $

Where to Stay

Holiday Inn Express, Highway 60 at Highway 2; (440) 967–8770; (888) 967–STAY. Conveniently located on Lake Erie, midway between Cedar Point and Cleveland, with **free** breakfast, indoor pool, sixty-six rooms, and a number of larger, family-style suites. $–$$

For More Information

Ottawa County Visitors Bureau, 770 Southeast Catawba Road, Port Clinton; (800) 441–1271; www.lake-erie.com.

Cleveland

Ohio's second-largest city, once jokingly referred to as the "mistake by the lake," is having the last laugh these days. Around the country a number of urban planners and envious city officials are pointing to Cleveland as the comeback city of the twentieth century.

Today it's also a sophisticated metropolis and a fascinating family destination. Despite an industrial bent, you'll find more than 19,000 acres of parkland and 90 miles of scenic Lake Erie shoreline, one of the country's finest art museums, and a renowned group of professional theaters for playgoers of all ages. Clevelanders are proud of their city, a five-time recipient of the prestigious All-American City Award. Recent headlines announced a new Marriott East hotel, which opened in September 2005. The city was also named in the top five for African-American families. For more on current events, weekend packages, and theater tickets, call the handy Visitor Information Hotline at (800) 321–1004 or log onto www.travelcleveland.com.

Lolly the Trolley (all ages)

1831 Columbus Road; (216) 771–4484, (800) 848–0173; www.lollytrolly.com.

Whenever you visit, a good way to get a handle on Cleveland's many offerings is to take one of the old-fashioned one- or two-hour Trolley Tours of downtown. Head for the Powerhouse on the west bank of the Flats, where you'll climb aboard one of five nostalgic, bright red trolleys, complete with carved oak interior, wrought-iron seat decoration, and the requisite clanging bell, and take in more than 20 miles of scenic stops and more than one hundred sights. All the trolleys are appropriately nicknamed

American Heritage Tour

Ohio and its residents played a key part in the African-American struggle for freedom prior to and during the Civil War. Some 50,000 to 75,000 fugitive slaves passed through the state on the Underground Railroad; during this time, dozens of "railroad lines" stretched from the banks of the Ohio River to the shores of Lake Erie.

Although former stations exist in virtually all regions of the state, few are as significant as Lorain County and the town of Oberlin, which has a specially designed African-American Heritage Tour available through the Lorain County Visitors Bureau. Oberlin gained notoriety as "the town that started the Civil War" when it harbored fugitive John Price during what later became known as the Oberlin-Wellington Slave Rescue of 1858.

Plaques now mark some of the famous rescue sites. In Oberlin many of the rescuers are buried in Westwood Cemetery, and many of the churches involved in the rescue, including the First Church of Oberlin, the meeting site for the Oberlin Antislavery Society, still stand. Don't miss the poignant Underground Railroad Memorial. Oberlin is also home to Oberlin College, the first American college to admit students "irrespective of color" in 1835.

Your kids may eschew the textbooks, but a visit here will bring history to life in a vivid, moving lesson they'll long remember.

For more information contact the Lorain County Visitors Bureau at (800) 334–1673 or visit www.lcvb.org.

"Lolly." (The company also owns Gus and Russ the Bus, Stan the Sedan, and Dan the Van.) There is also a series of special interest tours, such as Ethnic Markets and the Steeples and Spires church tour. Tickets range from $5.00 to $10.00 depending on the tour.

Goodtime III (all ages)

825 East Ninth Street; for tickets call (216) 861–5110 or www.goodtimeiii.com. Two-hour excursions depart daily at noon and 3:00 P.M. Memorial Day through Labor Day. Adults $$$, children ages two to eleven $$.

If you and your family are sailors, you might prefer getting your feet wet aboard the cruises offered by the quadruple-deck, 1,000-passenger *Goodtime III*, the city's largest sightseeing charter boat, and take in all the city sights along the river and lake. It sails from Cleveland's North Coast Harbor, next to the Rock and Roll Hall of Fame and the Great Lakes Science Center.

Don't forget to bring your camera. You'll enjoy a fast-changing panorama of vistas and views as the skyline passes. There are also popular dinner and dinner-dance cruises.

Nautica Queen (ages 4 and up) ⚠

1153 Main Avenue; (216) 696–8888, (800) 837–0604; www.nauticaqueen.com. Both cruises operate April through New Year's Eve, weather permitting. Adults $$$$, kids ages twelve and under $$$.

Sightseeing cruises also are offered by the elegant *Nautica Queen,* part of the Nautica Entertainment Complex, which offers daily lunch and dinner departures as well as a Sunday brunch. Most families opt for the popular luncheon cruise on Saturday, which features a groaning-board buffet of beef or chicken entree, pasta Alfredo, pasta marinara, mixed greens, dessert, and more. The ship is docked on the west bank of The Flats in downtown.

Steamship *William G. Mather* Museum (ages 3 and up) 🚢

Dock 32, North Coast Harbor; (216) 574–6262; www.wgmather.nhlink.net. Tours offered daily June through August and on weekends in May, September, and October. $

Steamship lovers can climb aboard the *William G. Mather* for another look at life on the high seas. The former flagship of the Cleveland Cliffs Iron Company is now a floating discovery center. At 618 feet, it was built in 1925 to carry ore, coal, and grain throughout the Great Lakes but now houses exhibits and displays that focus on the history and lore of these "iron boats." Would-be sailors are escorted through the pilothouse, the crew and guest quarters, and the galley as well as the guest and officers' dining room. A favorite of most kids is the huge, four-story engine room. In 2005 the museum moved to North Coast Harbor Park, near the Great Lakes Science Center, as part of the ongoing lakefront revitalization.

U.S.S. *Cod*

Docked at 1089 North Marginal Road, near the Burke Lakefront Airport; (216) 566–8770; www.usscod.org. Open daily 10:00 A.M. to 5:00 P.M. May through September. Adults $$, children $.

Prefer to go *under* the water? Indulge your undersea adventurers with a visit to the U.S.S. *Cod.* This World War II submarine—the last original and intact model left from a onetime fleet of more than 200—offers a real submarine-style experience. The 312-foot *Cod* is credited with seven successful war patrols that sank more than 27,000 tons of Imperial Japanese shipping. When it was retired from reserve training in 1976, it was saved from the scrap pile by a dedicated group of local veterans. Visitors are taken through the submarine's eight compartments and given demonstrations on its works as well as a lively history of life on board. A cool virtual tour can also be had on their Web site.

Ohio in **Cyberspace**

A good resource for information on the state's large cities and other attractions is Ohio's official tourism Web site: www.discoverohio.com. You'll find all the latest on attractions, events, accommodations, and more, all in an easy-to-follow format. There's also a section for kids, with lots of fun things to do and explore. While online, don't miss the chance to send an Ohio e-mail postcard, download a free screen saver, and enter the monthly contest.

Rock and Roll Hall of Fame and Museum (ages 5 and up; especially suited for older kids)

1 Key Plaza; (216) 781–7625 (ROCK), (888) 588–ROCK; www.rockhall.com. Open 10:00 A.M. to 5:30 P.M. daily; Wednesday until 9:00 P.M. $$$, children ages eight and under **free.**

If you opt to explore the city via your own two feet, better first put on your dancing shoes. Your first stop should be the Rock and Roll Hall of Fame downtown. Located along Cleveland's North Coast Harbor (not far from where the *Goodtime III* is docked), this stunning design includes a 165-foot tower that rises from the water and a variety of geometric shapes that explode from the tower, along with a shimmering, seven-story triangular-shaped glass tent.

Boogie on over and get ready to rock around the clock. After a national competition and years of planning, the 150,000-square-foot hall of fame and museum opened in September 1995. Internationally acclaimed architect I. M. Pei (known for his controversial addition to the Louvre Museum in Paris) designed the museum to be as groundbreaking and far-reaching as the musical style it honors.

City fathers claimed that Cleveland was the most appropriate place for the museum all along, since legendary disk jockey Alan Freed coined the term *rock 'n' roll* here during a 1951 broadcast. The city also served as the site of the first rock concert, the Moon Dog Coronation Ball, held in 1952.

The museum tells the story of *rock 'n' roll* from its roots in country, blues, R&B, and jazz to the latest forms of hip-hop and rap. Among the more than 4,000 artifacts in the permanent collection are the black leather outfit worn by Elvis Presley in his 1968 television special; John Lennon's *Sgt. Pepper's Lonely Hearts Club Band* uniform; original recording equipment from Sun Studios in Memphis; handwritten lyrics by Chuck Berry and Jimi Hendrix; Jim Morrison's Cub Scout uniform; Roy Orbison's sunglasses; and more. Exhibits include one devoted to Elvis—the largest exhibit on the King outside Memphis—and Beat & Rhymes, which explores the origins of hip-hop and rap. Newer exhibits include 500 Songs that Shaped Rock 'n' Roll, Music of Ohio, and Les Paul and the Electric Guitar. Recent traveling exhibitions have included

Tommy: the Amazing Journey and Listen to the Music: The Evolution of Audio Technology.

Some of this may seem like ancient history to your kids, but they can't help but be excited by the exhibits that let them host a live radio broadcast or see the recording booths that show how hit songs are created and recorded. The 50,000 square feet of exhibit space also features a jukebox with more than 27,000 songs, as well as lively displays and memorabilia. (But be forewarned: Your young music fans won't be able to resist poking fun at the way things were when you were young.)

Great Lakes Science Center (ages 5 and up) 🔵

601 Erieside Avenue; (216) 694–2000; www.glsc.org. Hours are 9:30 A.M. to 5:30 P.M. Monday through Saturday and 11:00 A.M. to 7:00 P.M. Sunday. Adults $$$, children ages three to seventeen $$.

Just steps away is the $54.9 million, 165,000-square-foot Great Lakes Science Center, also located on the section of Lake Erie known as the North Coast Harbor. In the nine years it has been open, it has rapidly become one of the most innovative science centers in the world. The center welcomed its five millionth visitor in July 2005 with a trip to Mars—Mars, Pennsylvania, that is—and a lifetime family membership.

Designed to provide a comprehensive learning center, it features 340 hands-on exhibits in 50,000 square feet that encourage young and old visitors alike to have fun while they learn. Features include a 20,000-square-foot gallery devoted to traveling and seasonal exhibits; an intriguing S.E.T. Piece, which concentrates on major themes of science, environment, and technology; a six-story, 320-seat domed OMNIMAX Theater (the region's only IMAX); and another sure hit: a riveting replica of the NASA mission-control station in Houston. Highlights include an indoor tornado, a bridge of fire, and more. There is also a variety of special traveling exhibits. Recent offerings included Hexagon, Marbles, Harmonious Waves, and Elliptical Pool Tables, an unusual game of chance.

West Side Market 🍴

1995 West Twenty-fifth Street; (216) 664–3387; www.westsidemarket.com.

A great place for an impromptu and always fresh meal is the historic West Side Market, located at West Twenty-fifth Street and Lorain Avenue. Duck inside the door of this vintage 1912 Old World–style market—one of the largest and last in the United States—and you'll be overwhelmed by the smells of exotic meats and cheeses, fresh baked goods, and more. It's definitely an attraction as well as a tempting eatery.

More than one hundred indoor and outdoor merchants from a variety of ethnic groups serve up anything your family's hearts desire in a friendly, carnival-type setting. Not surprisingly, kids often opt for hot dogs—some of the best in the city—from one of the many vendors.

The **Flats**

The city's waterfront is also home to the Flats, a restored area located along the Cleveland Memorial Shoreway. Once the home of hundreds of heavy industries, the Flats is now the city's premier entertainment district and is home to more than fifty restaurants and nightclubs. An interesting mix of converted warehouses dots the east and west banks of the area, where the Cuyahoga River meets Lake Erie.

The popular Nautica Entertainment Complex covers some twenty-eight acres on the river's west bank and includes a 4,100-seat amphitheater, a riverfront boardwalk, and a floating restaurant. Anchored by two jackknife bridges, the complex has attracted millions of people since it opened in 1987. Pig out on pasta at the Spaghetti Warehouse, a family favorite. You can even dine in a trolley car. Afterward, if your offspring are into sing-alongs, buy them a soda and check out the fun at the rollicking Howl at the Moon Saloon. Dueling baby grands and TV theme songs make this a popular spot with teenagers and college students.

The complex is also home to the popular Cleveland Cool KidsFest, an outdoor festival just for kids that's held each July. Special entertainment, sports, rides, activities, games, and more make up this weekend of fun for all ages. For more information call (216) 247–2722.

The district really heats up at night, when the nightclubs host big-name entertainment from all over the country, but it's a pleasant place for an alfresco family lunch anytime and a great spot to watch passing freighters, some of which are up to 600 feet long and fly flags from all over the world. Even landlubbers love listening to the freighters boom their horn blasts of greeting as they pass each other. It's also home to the city's rowing clubs, which can be seen in warmer months. The Flats Racing League now has more than 1,200 members.

Jacobs Field (ages 4 and up) 🕸
2401 Ontario Street; for tickets, call (216) 420–4200; www.indians.com.

If you're a family of sports lovers, Cleveland is your town. From the excitement of a buzzer shot at a Cavs game to a summer day at an Indians game, Cleveland offers enough thrills to satisfy sportsaholics of any age.

Catch an Indians game at Jacobs Field in the heart of downtown. This state-of-the-art facility holds 42,000-plus screaming fans, who come to experience the thrills of America's favorite pastime and enjoy spectacular views of the field and skyline as well as of the largest freestanding scoreboard in North America.

Jacobs Field is part of the city's world-class sports and entertainment complex that opened in 1994. Located downtown on the site of the twenty-eight-acre Old Central Market, Gateway Ballpark and Arena has gained international attention for its visionary design and its two arenas—the aforementioned $161 million, 42,865-seat Jacobs Field and Quicken Loans Arena, a $118 million, 20,750-seat indoor arena, home of the Cleveland Cavaliers NBA basketball team, the Lumberjacks hockey team, and the Thunderbolts arena football team. Quicken Loans Arena also has concerts and family-oriented special events.

The ballpark is a mere five-minute stroll from most downtown hotels and is connected by a walkway to Tower City Center. With panoramic views of the city's skyline, a restaurant that looks out over the playing field, food courts, and tempting team gift shops as well as a collection of colorful public art by noted regional artists, Gateway is sure to score with young fans. Tours are offered in season from the Team Shop every half hour from 10:00 A.M. to 2:00 P.M. Monday through Saturday.

Candy Tours (ages 3 and up)

Chocoholics of all ages are in for a treat in Cleveland. Two local candy companies—Malley's Chocolates in Cleveland and Olympia Gourmet Chocolates and Corn in nearby suburban Strongsville—offer tours and, of course, **free** samples of their gooey goodies. At Malley's—the city's largest family-owned and operated chocolate factory—you'll hear the story of chocolate and see nuts roasted, chocolates dipped, molds filled, and fancy packages wrapped. The factory is at 13400 Brookpark Road; call (800) 275–6255 or (216) 226–8300.

Ever see the episode of the *I Love Lucy* show in which Lucy does a stint at a chocolate factory? Don a hair net, apron, and surgical gloves and see for yourself what it's like at Olympia Gourmet Chocolates (for a price, of course—for $300, you and twelve of your closest friends can experience the candy assembly line firsthand). Olympia, which has been around for more than eighty years, specializes in gourmet chocolate candy and caramel corn. Visitors get in on the action during the two-hour tours and help make their signature chocolate goodies. Afterward, you can fill up a box with your favorite creations. **Free** tours are offered depending on demand; reservations are necessary. Olympia is at 11606 Pearl Road, Strongsville; call (440) 572–7747.

Amazing
Ohio Facts

Ohio's nickname is the Buckeye State.

Ohio's state flower is the scarlet carnation.

Playhouse Square Center (ages 5 and up, depending on production)

1501 Euclid Avenue; (216) 771–4444; www.playhousesquare.com.

Although sports are a big ticket in Cleveland, many visitors are surprised to discover that the arts draw even larger crowds. While professional sports brought in $79 million in the early 1990s, the arts added some $190.5 million to the city's coffers.

Of the city's many arts lovers, nearly 25 percent line up for the city's live theater. Cleveland is considered Broadway's home away from home, with many major shows either debuted or coproduced here. Recent productions have included *Wicked, Little Shop of Horrors, Amadeus, As You Like It,* and the family favorite *The Nutcracker.* It's a great place to introduce your offspring to the magic of the greasepaint without the sticker shock you'll find these days on the Great White Way, where good seats can easily cost $100.

The cornerstone of Cleveland theater is Playhouse Square, now the largest performing arts center outside New York City, with more than 10,000 seats and nearly a million annual patrons of all ages. Playhouse Square boasts five renovated theaters, all of which are worth visiting for a **free** tour, even if nothing's on stage.

The spectacular Ohio, State, Palace, and Allen Theaters, all of which were originally built in the 1920s as vaudeville palaces, were converted in the 1950s to movie houses and fell into disrepair in the late 1960s. After a long fund-raising drive, Playhouse Square became home to five resident companies: the Cleveland Opera, the Ohio Ballet, Dance Cleveland, Tri-C Jazz Fest, and The Broadway Series. Children's series include the Children's Theatre Series for ages three to eight and the Discovery series for ages eight to twelve. Performances range from *A Christmas Carol* to *A Midsummer Night's Dream.*

Move Over, **Lincoln Center**

Upon completion of Playhouse Square Center's most recent renovation, Cleveland became home to the nation's second-largest performing arts center, behind only New York City's Lincoln Center.

Cleveland Play House (ages 5 and up, depending on production) 🎵
8500 Euclid Avenue; (216) 795–7000; www.clevelandplayhouse.com.

Another long-standing Cleveland theatrical tradition is the Cleveland Play House. Founded in 1915, it celebrated its ninetieth season in 2005 as the oldest nonprofit professional theater in the country. It specializes in producing favorites as well as original plays. Recent productions include *The Legend of Johnny Appleseed* and *The Emperor's New Clothes*. The Play House stages three children's plays each year for elementary school–age children.

Karamu House (ages 5 and up, depending on production) 🎵
2355 East Eighty-ninth Street; (216) 795–7070; www.karamu.com.

Also founded in 1915, the Karamu House is the oldest African-American theater in the country (translated from Swahili, *Karamu* means "place of enjoyment"). The multiracial, multicultural theater pioneered interracial theater in its early days and featured the works of many unknown Black playwrights. There's also an early childhood development center, with a great summer program, a cultural arts and education center, and a full roster of special events.

University Circle District

The arts also take center stage in University Circle, about 4 miles east of downtown. Just 1 mile long, the area is home to internationally renowned museums; performing arts centers; and music, art, and educational institutions—the largest concentration of its kind in the country. All are within walking distance of one another and are situated in a relaxing, parklike setting of manicured gardens and winding boulevards. For general information call (216) 791–3900 or log onto www.universitycircle.org.

Falling for **Chagrin Falls**

You've done the Rock and Roll Hall of Fame, taken a spin on a trolley tour, and explored the Nautica Entertainment Complex. When your gang's tired of the tourist track, head for Chagrin Falls, east of downtown.

Although it's officially a suburb of Cleveland, Chagrin Falls feels like a small New England village. There are charming shops, good lunch spots, and a vintage sweet shop where you can pick up a few goodies to enjoy in the park across the way. During a recent visit, my kids had fun just kicking back, feeding the ducks on the river that runs through the center of town, and ogling the scenic falls that give the city its name. For information call (440) 247–6607.

Cleveland Museum of Art (all ages) 🖼

11150 East Boulevard; (216) 421–7340, (888) 262–0033; www.clevelandart.org. Open from 10:00 A.M. to 5:00 P.M. Tuesday, Thursday, Saturday, and Sunday and 10:00 A.M. to 9:00 P.M. Wednesday and Friday. Free.

This three-story classical structure, named "one of the nation's premier collections" by the *New York Times,* is currently undergoing a $258-million renovation and expansion, with most of the excellent permanent collection in storage. While the museum is not expected to fully reopen until early 2007, it will continue to host traveling exhibitions. A recent offering included The Arts and Crafts Movement in Europe and America: 1880–1920: Design for a Modern World. Watch the museum's Web site for construction updates.

Children's Museum of Cleveland (all ages) 🖼

10730 Euclid Avenue; (216) 791–5437; www.clevelandchildrensmuseum.org. Open 10:00 A.M. to 5:00 P.M. Tuesday through Saturday; noon to 5:00 P.M. Sunday.

"Please Touch" could be the motto of the innovative Cleveland Children's Museum on Euclid Avenue in University Circle. More like an activity center than a museum, it houses more than one hundred displays that the whole gang can enjoy. Get wet—or at least learn about the properties of water—at Water, Water Everywhere, which explores the mysteries of water and its cycles as children pour and pump, carve riverbanks, work waterwheels, draw fish, and enjoy racing a boat along a replica of Lake Erie.

Prefer heights? Enter a deep forest to check out Tales in Tall Trees, which encourages story making and an understanding of the role of storytelling in many cultures. A maze, puppets, dioramas, and a gallery of wild beasts are just a few of the things on hand to foster wonder, imagination, and play. Other "old favorites" include the Over and Under Bridges area, where child-size bridges can be worked by little hands; and the popular People Puzzle, which lets kids create their own self-portraits, compare diverse features, play with puppets, and try their hand at being a roving reporter.

The museum is also the site of Healthier Ever After, an active fairy-tale forest that teaches children about their bodies and healthy nutrition. The new exhibit features a Stretching Station, Move and Groove Meadow, Crocodile Crossing, Pedal Pond, Coordination Cave, and Healthier Ever After Castle. Afterward, visit the Goodness Grove, where children learn about the importance of eating fruits and veggies. Other worthvisiting exhibitions include the wet and wild Splish, Splash; Bridges to Our Community; and the ever-popular Bed Red Barn, filled with fun hands-on activities.

Cleveland Museum of Natural History (all ages) 🖼

1 Wade Oval Drive; (216) 231–4600, (800) 317–9155; www.cmnh.org. Open 10:00 A.M. to 5:00 P.M. Monday through Saturday (until 10:00 P.M. on Wednesday, September through May), Sunday noon to 5:00 P.M. Adults $$, seniors and children ages seven to eighteen $, under seven free.

Want to have light-years of fun in a single day? Head for the Cleveland Museum of Natural History, Ohio's largest natural science museum, also located in University Circle. The Barney set loves the dinosaurs and other prehistoric creatures; the birds, botany, and geology exhibits; and the fascinating Hall of Man, home to "Lucy," the three-million-year-old skeleton of the oldest known human. You'll be welcomed by "Steggie," an 18-foot-long, 8-foot-high, plate-backed dino sculpture.

Regarded as one of the finest in North America, the museum is housed in a modern, 200,000-square-foot facility and draws 400,000 visitors annually. Many come to see the Foucault Pendulum in the main lobby, which demonstrates the rotation of Earth. It's the world's only pendulum in which the electromagnet that keeps the 270-pound bob moving is placed underneath rather than mounted on the top.

Special events have included Glacial Erratica, exploring the natural features of Kelleys Island; What's New; and Discovering Chimpanzees: The Remarkable World of Jane Goodall, which runs through September 2006.

Kids of all interests ooh and aah at Happy, the skeleton of a 70-foot-long haplocanthosaurus, one of the oldest sauropods on display anywhere in the world. Younger movie fans (including my daughter, Claire) appreciate the display cases occupied by the legendary Balto, also a Disney favorite. See stars in the planetarium, and come nose to nose with native animals and wildlife in the outdoor environmental courtyard or rustic wood garden. Browse in the well-stocked gift shop, cleverly named the Ark in the Park.

Western Reserve Historical Society/Crawford Auto-Aviation Museum (all ages) 🚗♿

10825 East Boulevard; (216) 721–5722; www.wrhs.org. Open 10:00 A.M. to 5:00 P.M. Monday through Saturday and noon to 5:00 P.M. Sunday. $$, children under six are free.

History of another kind lives on at the Western Reserve Historical Society, Cleveland's oldest cultural institution. It was founded in 1867 to preserve and promote the rich heritage of northeast Ohio.

Baseball, roller coasters, classic cars, bowling machines, airplanes, log cabins, and more are crammed into this collection, which captures the area's diverse past. Browse among the costumes, farming tools, manuscripts, and period rooms that recreate the area known as the Western Reserve from the pre–Revolutionary War era through the early twentieth century.

The centerpiece of the museum is the Hay-McKinney mansion, built in 1911 and designed by the son of President James Garfield. The ornate Italian Florentine–style villa is filled with important period furniture and decorative arts and once was part of the city's "Millionaires' Row" that stretched along part of Euclid Avenue. (The mayor's home located here even boasted an indoor ice-skating rink.) Tours offered daily every half hour from noon to 5:00 P.M. also take you "downstairs" to the servants' quarters for a starkly different view of nineteenth-century life.

Twinkle, **twinkle**

The Shafran Planetarium, the Cleveland Museum's latest addition, is one of the best in the nation. Its unique design allows it to function as an astronomical instrument; its chamfered roof helps nighttime visitors locate the North Star. The Skymaster ZKP3/S projector is the first of its kind in the world and can show the position of more than 5,000 stars, nebulae, and galaxies.

Car buffs of all ages flock to the society's Crawford Auto-Aviation Museum, which houses more than 200 streamlined, vintage, and classic automobiles and aircraft, including a rare collection of Cleveland-built cars. The collection will move to the waterfront in late 2006 or early 2007, when the new Crawford Museum of Transportation and Industry opens. Especially popular with little (and big) boys, it's considered one of the finest collections in the nation. Non-car buffs get equal time at the Chisholm Hall Costume Wing, where kids' clothes, men's suits, hats, shoes, and more encourage dress-up fantasies and make the wing the best-dressed tourist attraction in town. Everyone likes a stroll down the re-created turn-of-the-twentieth-century Street of Shops. There are also a number of special exhibits, including Millionaires' Row and Ice Cream: The Whole Scoop.

Cleveland Metroparks Zoo (all ages)

3900 Wildlife Way; (216) 661–6500; www.clemetzoo.com. The zoo is open daily from 10:00 A.M. to 5:00 P.M.; until 7:00 P.M. from Memorial Day through Labor Day. Adults $$, children ages two to eleven $.

The Cleveland Metroparks Zoo is home to the largest collection of primate species in North America. Thousands of animals roam the 168 outdoor acres and 2 indoor acres known as the RainForest, a groundbreaking exhibit that opened in 1992.

Under a domed, copper-colored glass structure that covers two floors and some 80,000 square feet, the RainForest gives refuge to more than 600 animals from more than 118 species that are in the process of losing or have lost their natural habitats. There are also more than 10,000 plants from 360 different varieties and 65 different plant families housed here.

In many ways, it's like a modern-day Noah's Ark. There are small-clawed otters, ocelots, dwarf crocodiles, golden lion monkeys, Puerto Rican crested toads, and even Dumeril ground boas. Many of the species found here have never been seen at a zoo.

As you wander along paths lined with low, leafy plants and orchid-studded trees, a continuous soundtrack plays recordings made in real rain forests. Nearby, a 30-foot indoor waterfall pours 90,000 gallons of recycled water per minute, sending beads of water into air that is already kept at an eighty-degree temperature with 80 percent humidity. The climax of your visit is a series of rain-forest storms, complete with heart-pounding thunder, blinding lightning, and overhead rain. You can't help but be moved as you watch a video of bulldozers and chain saws tear away at the soil as you near the exhibition's exit.

Although RainForest is still among the zoo's most popular attractions, the zoo is also home to more than 3,000 other animals, birds, and fish living in simulated natural habitats. You'll see ostriches, zebras, and giraffes in Africa and sharks, lungfish, and piranhas in the aquatics area. Kangaroos and wallabies populate the lands known as Australasia, where you can hop on the Outback Railroad for a tour. Other highlights include Birds of Prey, Public Greenhouse, and the Rhinoceros/Cheetah area. New in 2001 was Australian Adventure, an eight-acre early-learning experience for children ages three to twelve. It includes Koala Junction, Wallaby Walkabout, and Kookaburra Station and is designed to teach children about Australian wildlife and the inner workings of an Australian ranch.

New in 2004 was the $9.1 million Sarah Allison Steffee Center for Zoological Medicine, which serves the zoo animals' veterinary needs. The adjacent Reinberger Learning Lab shows visitors behind-the-scenes views of zoo animal care.

NASA John Glenn Research Center Visitor Center
(ages 5 and up)

21000 Brookpark Road; (216) 433–2000; www.lerc.nasa.gov/. Open 9:00 A.M. to 4:00 P.M. weekdays, 10:00 A.M. to 3:00 P.M. Saturday, and 1:00 to 5:00 P.M. Sunday. Free.

You'll definitely get a head rush from a visit to the NASA Visitor Center, not far from the airport, where the "final frontier" is the focus. It's up, up, and away at one of the country's most advanced research facilities, one of just ten such centers in the United States, the only one in the Midwest, and the only NASA facility north of the Mason-Dixon Line.

With programs in aeronautics and space-age technology, NASA Glenn at Lewis Field is also home to the Microgravity Materials Science Laboratory, a facility used to test potential space experiments; a zero-gravity drop tower; wind tunnels; space environment tanks; and chambers for testing jet-engine efficiency and noise.

All this and more is explored in a fascinating 6,000-square-foot, six-gallery visitor center. Here amateur astronauts head for the authentic Apollo/Skylab capsule, the Lunar Lander computer game, and various other exhibits that trace the history of space exploration. The center opened its doors to the public in 1976 and has welcomed more than 100,000 visitors each year since.

In six exhibition galleries you'll find a variety of educational and informative programs on aeronautics, space exploration, the solar system, air and spacecraft propulsion, the Space Shuttle and the *Apollo Skylab III* Command Module, satellites, materials and structures research, and spinoffs of NASA programs. Other highlights include a tribute to John Glenn and an exploration of space communications. A popular lecture series focuses on topics related to aeronautics, such as "Space Basics 101" and "Fostering Your Daughter's Enjoyment and Success in Math, Science, and Engineering." The auditorium features special videos related to recent NASA shuttle missions. Across from the visitor center you'll also find large examples of the 15,775-pound Agena Rocket; the 800-pound Ranger, designed to broadcast pictures from the moon; and the Centaur Rocket, used on planetary and satellite launches since 1966.

If your kids are teenagers, consider the insider's view of the research center's activities offered on Wednesday afternoon from 2:00 to 3:00 P.M. (no one under age sixteen is admitted). *NOTE:* Due to increased security concerns, proof of citizenship and a photo I.D. are required for all adults. Tours visit the flight research building, the propulsion systems lab, the zero-gravity facility, and the 10- by 10-foot supersonic wind tunnel. Reservations are required.

International Women's Air & Space Museum (ages 6 and up)

1501 North Marginal Road; (216) 623–1111; www.iwasm.org. Hours vary with day and season. **Free.**

If girls seem to get short shrift at NASA, check out this small museum dedicated to women's achievements in aviation and space. Located in Burke Lakefront Airport terminal, it has a research center and small gift shop. The museum moved from the Dayton area, but still honors women's role in aviation and space history. Among the recognized aviators are Amelia Earhart, Jacqueline Cochran, women astronauts, and even women involved in Operation Desert Storm. A special display honors Katharine Wright, Wilbur and Orville's sister. Katharine has been mostly forgotten, but Orville once said "When the world speaks of the Wrights, it must include my sister, for much of our effort has been inspired by her."

Where to Eat

The city has plenty of fairly priced family spots. My family's favorites include:

Guarino's, 12309 Mayfield Road; (216) 231–3100. If your kids are clamoring for Italian, check out this eatery in the city's Little Italy. The city's oldest restaurant, it features lots of family-pleasing pasta dishes, all fresh and flavorful. $–$$

Hornblower's Barge & Grill, 1151 North Marginal Road; (216) 363–1151. This floating restaurant has water views and a nice children's menu, but it is better suited for kids ages four and up. $$

100th Bomb Group—A Restaurant, 20000 Brookpark Road; (216) 267–1010. Although not cheap, this French farmhouse setting with a World War II aviation theme delights would-be pilots both big and small. $$

Spaghetti Warehouse, 1231 Main Avenue; (216) 621–9240. This reliable family pleaser features a variety of pastas and an interior loaded with vintage style. $$

If you're staying in the suburbs, there are also **Olive Garden Italian Restaurants,** a chain, in Middleburg Heights, North Olmstead, and Parma.

Where to Stay

Courtyard by Marriott, 5051 West Creek Road; (216) 901–9988. Although a little farther outside the city center in suburban Independence, this clean and well-run chain hotel is a great place for families, with 154 rooms, a pool, and a great breakfast bar. $–$$

Holiday Inn Select City Center, 1111 Lakeside Avenue; (216) 241–5100. This centrally located, family-oriented hotel has 380 rooms, eighteen stories, an indoor pool, and more. $$

Hyatt Regency Cleveland at the Arcade, 420 Superior Avenue; (800) 233–1234. When you want a treat, head for this historic charmer. It took eighteen months to restore the century-old site to its original grandeur. It has 293 rooms, a restaurant, a wine bar, a pool, and shops. $$$

Residence Inn, 5101 West Creek Road; (216) 520–1450. If you're looking for room to spread out, it's worth the drive to suburban Independence, not far from downtown. The inn has 118 spacious suites, 28 with two bedrooms. $$

For More Information

Cleveland Convention and Visitors Bureau, Suite 3100, Terminal Tower, 50 Public Square, Cleveland 44113; (800) 321–1004; www.travelcleveland.com.

Geneva-on-the-Lake

Looking for a trip back in time? Longing for those simpler days of summer that you remember from your own youth? The lakeside community of Geneva-on-the-Lake, known nostalgically as "Ohio's First Summer Resort," offers a trip down memory lane.

The mile-long strip provides plenty of classic cuisine, including foot-longs, hamburgers, french fries, and ice cream, and a variety of nightspots, eateries, and amusements. Three of the oldest are Eddie's Grill, a local favorite for more than fifty years; Madsen's Donuts, which has served up gooey treats since 1938; and Erieview Amusement Park, which has entertained families for more than a century. Although the old-time casino and pier ballroom are gone, lively entertainment can still be had on the outdoor patio of the Old Firehouse Winery. Other area options include water slides, arcades, and the oldest miniature golf course in the United States in continuous play. Or you could just grab an inner tube (for rent on the pier) and spend a day frolicking in the surf.

Although you won't find the Victorian bed-and-breakfasts that are abundant in some other Ohio communities, there are plenty of campgrounds, cabins, and cottages for rent.

For more information on hotels and restaurants, call the Geneva-on-the-Lake Convention and Visitors Bureau at (440) 466–8600 or visit www.ncweb.com/gol.

Kirtland

Lake Farm Park (all ages) 🏕️ 🐘 🦋 🔒

8800 Chardon Road; (440) 256–2122, (800) 366–FARM (3276); www.lakemetroparks
.com. Open 9:00 A.M. to 5:00 P.M. daily. Adults $$, children ages two to eleven $.

A little science. A little history. A lot of fun. The brochure for Lake Farm Park, an open-air science and cultural center just east of downtown Cleveland, says it all. With 235 acres of fields and forests, a barnyard area with more than fifty breeds of livestock (including more than a dozen endangered breeds), wagon and sleigh rides, antique tractors, and more, it's a city kid's country fantasy come true.

Teach your horticulturists- or farmers-to-be with a visit to the hydroponic greenhouse displays or the strange-but-wonderful Great Tomato Works, billed as "the world's most unusual horticultural science exhibit."

The Great Tomato Works includes the world's largest tomato hornworm and the world's largest tomato plant, with vines as big as your waist, fruit 6 feet across, and leaves up to 12 feet long. The display also explores the life processes of plants and food production, including hands-on exhibits that show how plants make sugar from sunshine, how roots store water, and how tomatoes are transformed into ketchup. Other highlights include a Dairy Parlor, where would-be farmers can test their milking skills.

The farm is also the spot for fun at year-round festivals, including the Woolly World Fest in May, a Fall Harvest in September, and the ever-popular Farmpark Sheepdog Challenge in November. Afterward, stop for a bite at the Calf-A restaurant.

Holden Arboretum (all ages) 🚶 🎮 🦋

9500 Sperry Road; (440) 946–4400; www.holdenarb.org. Open Sunday through Thursday from 10:00 A.M. to 4:45 P.M.; Friday and Saturday 10:00 A.M. to 6:45 P.M. $, children under six are free.

Looking to get back to nature? Kirtland is also home to the largest arboretum in the United States. Holden Arboretum is a 3,100-acre preserve of natural woodlands, horticultural collections, display gardens, walking trails, ponds, and open fields. Plants include rhododendrons, crab apple, maples, conifers, nut trees, wildflowers, lilacs, and viburnums. This is a great place to wind down and explore the wilderness. After a stop at the informative visitor center, explore the nearby butterfly garden, take to the trails, or enjoy an alfresco meal at the scenic picnic area on the grounds.

Fairport Harbor Lakefront Beach Park (all ages) 🌊 🚗 🏛️

(800) 227–PARK (7275); www.dnr.state.oh.us/parks. Open dawn to dusk. Free.

Need to cool off? The new kid on the block in Lake County is the Fairport Harbor Lakefront Beach Park. This twenty-acre, $1.6 million beach is definitely worth a stop—and a dip; stock up on the sunscreen and load up the picnic basket. You'll find long stretches of sandy beach, concession stands, playgrounds, picnic areas, water-equipment-rental businesses, and even a lighthouse museum, all part of Headlands Beach State Park.

Jefferson/Ashtabula

Covered Bridge Festival (ages 2 and up)

25 West Jefferson Street; (440) 576–3769; www.coveredbridgefestival.org. Adults $, free for kids ages twelve and younger.

Continue to skirt Lake Erie, and eventually you'll end up in Ashtabula County, best known as the covered-bridge capital of Ohio. Who needs Madison County when Ashtabula has a record fifteen covered bridges of its own?

From the Creek Road Covered Bridge, which has an unknown date of construction, to Harpersfield Covered Bridge, the longest in the state of Ohio and a designated National Historic Site, Ashtabula is proud of its bridges and heritage. So proud, in fact, that it now has a Covered Bridge Festival each year on the second weekend in October, held at the Ashtabula County Fairgrounds.

Antique engines and tractors, a Civil War encampment, a parade, and covered-bridge tours are just a few of the highlights. Children love the scarecrow contest, Ding-a-Ling Train Rides, the draft-horse pull, the plowing contest, and lively entertainment.

A C & J Scenic Line (ages 4 and up)

East Jefferson Street; (440) 576–8848; www.acjrailroad.com. $$

Enjoy a one-hour, 12-mile round-trip family train ride on one of the last remaining NYC "High Grade" line trains that ran from Ashtabula to Pittsburgh, Pennsylvania. Three restored vintage coaches pulled by a first-generation diesel locomotive offer regular departures on weekends June through October. There's also a Santa Train in December. No reservations necessary.

The Victorian Perambulator Museum (ages 5 and up)

26 East Cedar Street; (440) 576–9588. Hours vary. Admission by donation.

Little girls will think they're in heaven here, with more than 200 examples of early wicker carriages, Victorian games, books, and toys.

Great Lakes Marine and U.S. Coast Guard Museum (ages 3 and up)

1071 Walnut Boulevard, Ashtabula Harbor; (440) 964–6847; www.ashtcohs.com/ashmus.html. Open noon to 5:00 P.M. Friday through Sunday in summer and 1:00 to 5:00 P.M. till the end of October. Donations accepted.

Make your way along historic Ashtabula Harbor to the Great Lakes Marine and U.S. Coast Guard Museum, where you can explore Great Lakes history. The small but charming museum is housed in the old lighthouse keeper's home, a duplex built in 1898. The U.S. Coast Guard took it over and used it as a station before it became a volunteer-run museum in 1984.

Today you can explore the seven rooms and a pilothouse from the 1911 *Thomas Walters,* an ore boat built in nearby Lorain. Small fry especially like the working radar and the rare working model of a hulett, an iron-ore unloading machine. Only four are left standing on Lake Erie today. There are also photographs, clothing, and other mementos of a sailor's life on the lake. An adjacent picnic area offers great views and plenty of photo opportunities.

Hubbard House Underground Railroad Museum

(ages 5 and up)

Walnut Boulevard and Lake Avenue; (440) 964–8168; www.hubbardhouseugrrmuseum .org. Open 1:00 to 5:00 P.M. Friday through Sunday May through September. $, children under six are **free.**

History buffs of all ages enjoy a visit to this 1841 home, one of the last stops for slaves traveling the Underground Railroad to Canada. Tours are led by Tim Hubbard, a descendant of the original owners.

Where to Eat

Casa Capelli, 4641 Main Avenue; (440) 992–3700. Housed in a former bank complete with stained glass, peaked ceilings, and a vault/dining room, this friendly restaurant specializes in Italian cuisine but also features Mexican and continental choices. $$

Covered Bridge Pizza, 380 East Main Street, Andover; (440) 293–6776; Highway 193, North Kingsville; (440) 224–0497; and 4861 North Ridge Road West, Ashtabula, (440) 969–1000. Covered bridges are so much a part of the area's psyche that there's even a pizza parlor in one. In 1972 Ashtabula County sold one of its covered bridges—formerly known as the Forman Road Bridge—for just $5.00. Today it's known as Covered Bridge Pizza and has three locations, one in neighboring

Kingsville, one in Ashtabula, and one in Andover. Dine in the bridge and enjoy homemade pizza, pasta, chili, sandwiches, and subs. $$

Hulbert's Restaurant, 1035 Bridge Street; (440) 964–0248. Cozy decor, including Victorian accents and tables resting on antique sewing-machine bases, complements the homemade soups and entrees. Known for fresh walleye, roast beef, and its local wine list. $$

For More Information

Ashtabula County Convention and Visitors Bureau, 1850 Austinburg Road, Austinburg 44010; (440) 275–3202, (800) 337–6746; www.accvb.org.

Twinsburg

Twins Days Festival (all ages)

(330) 425–3652. For more information contact the Twins Days Festival Committee, Inc., P.O. Box 29, Twinsburg 44807 or visit www.twinsdays.org. $

Don't blink . . . there's nothing wrong with your eyes. You'll be seeing lots of doubles during the annual Twins Days Festival, the largest gathering of twins in the world. Even the town, located along Interstate 480 about midway between Cleveland and Akron, was named for the more than 20,000 sets of identical and fraternal twins who congregate here the first full weekend in August each year. The festival was founded in 1976 as part of the city of Twinsburg's bicentennial festivities and commemorates town founders Moses and Aaron Wilcox, twin brothers who settled the town in the early 1800s.

This prime people-watching weekend has been featured in *Newsweek, Reader's Digest, People Magazine,* and on ABC's *World News Tonight.* It's listed in the *Guinness Book of World Records* as the largest gathering of twins. It has grown from just 37 sets of twins in 1976 to nearly 25,000 sets in 2000. In 2005 Maya and Miguel from the PBS Scholastic Channel visited, and the Discovery Channel filmed the festival as part of a feature on identical twins.

But you and your family don't have to have a double to enjoy the festival. Events include the Double-Take Parade, chock-full of twins, floats, and marching bands. Each day, twins participate in more than thirty-five twins contests, including most or least identical, oldest, youngest, farthest traveled, even widest combined smile. Besides all this, there's a variety of arts and crafts, rides for kids, games, food stands, exhibits, and entertainment. Other highlights include a twin fireworks display, group photos (there are so many attendees that they take them on a hill near the town), and more.

Where to Stay

Hilton Garden Inn, 8971 Wilcox Drive; (330) 405–4499. Upscale accommodations with pool, exercise room, laundry, and 142 newer rooms. $$

Twinsburg Super 8, 8848 Twins Hills Drive; (330) 425–2889. Comfortable two-story chain hotel with sixty rooms. $

Aurora

Geauga Lake and Wildwater Kingdom Family Amusement Park
(all ages) 🛒 😎 🐘
1060 North Aurora Road; (330) 562–7131; www.geaugalake.com. Hours vary with season. $$$$

After a series of owners that ranged from Sea World to Six Flags, this classic amusement park is now owned and operated by Cedar Fair, owners of Cedar Point.

The new owners have wasted no time in making changes, first of which is Wildwater Kingdom, one of the largest waterparks in the United States. Located on the fifty-six acres of the former Sea World, the $24-million waterpark opened in June 2005.

Each of Cedar Fair's parks offers something special. For Geauga Lake it's the waterpark, which will rank as one of the largest in the industry. Opening in two stages, the 2005 section includes a new 60-foot-tall funnel-shaped raft slide; a lazy river with a variety of wave generators and interactive spray gadgets; and the relocated Hurricane Mountain, Ohio's tallest waterslide complex. A new children's area will include an enormous tipping bucket that spills 1,000 gallons of water on guests every two minutes, as well as a children's pool with waterslides, bubblers, geysers, and spray gadgets. Teens aren't forgotten either; they can enjoy their own activity pool with net climbs, floating cargo crawling, bubbling pools, and more.

The 2006 addition will include a 38,000-square-foot wave pool, an adult pool with whirlpool spas, waterfalls, and a swim-up bar.

Other must-see attractions include wandering members of the *Peanuts* gang; a variety of classic roller coasters; a 3-D interactive film, *Robots of Mars;* and the Dino Island II motion simulator.

Where to Eat

Country Manor, 1225 West Main Street, Kent; (330) 673–0222. Casual family dining with a children's menu and a popular Sunday brunch. $

Pufferbelly LTD, 152 Franklin Avenue, Kent; (330) 673–1771. A railroad fan's favorite, this eatery, located in the old Kent Railway Depot, is just west of town in the historic district. Kids' menu; Sunday brunch. $–$$

Where to Stay

Bertram Inn, 600 North Aurora Road; (330) 995–0200, (877) 995–0200. Newer inn and conference center (opened March 2000) features 162 rooms and suites, amusement park packages, a surprising sushi bar, and more. $$

Walden, The Country Inn and Stables, 1119 Aurora Hudson Road; (330) 562–5508; www.waldenco.com. Smaller inn with twenty-five rooms, five with family-style kitchens. Horseback riding, **free** breakfast, and more. $$

Ohio's **National Road**

Now in its second printing, *A Traveler's Guide to the Historic National Road in Ohio: The Road That Helped Build America* is available free of charge from the Ohio Historical Society. The forty-six-page full-color guide provides a point-by-point description of the significant historical, cultural, natural and recreational sites associated with the National Road in Ohio. The route generally follows modern U.S. Highway 40 and in some areas parallels Interstate 70. Clusters of historic buildings, stone bridges, taverns, inns, vintage service stations, eateries, and accommodations stand as reminders of an earlier time when the National Road was "the Main Street of America."

The National Road in Ohio is part of a six-state All American Road, National Scenic Byway, that stretches more than 700 miles from Baltimore through Maryland, Pennsylvania, Ohio, Indiana, and Illinois. In Ohio the National Road runs 227 miles from Belmont County in the east to Preble County in the west, traveling through rural areas, towns, and urban Columbus along the way.

In 2006 the National Road will celebrates the 200th anniversary of its authorization by Congress as the nation's first federally funded interstate.

For your copy of the guide or for more information, visit www.ohio history.org, or call (800) 686–6124.

Peninsula Area

Cuyahoga Valley National Recreation Area (all ages)

For a National Park Service brochure, contact 15610 Vaughn Road, Brecksville 44141; (440) 526–5256; www.nps.gov/cuva. Hours for visitor center: 8:00 A.M. to 5:00 P.M. daily; the remainder is open dawn to dusk. **Free.**

Seven million visitors each year can't be wrong. That's the number of travelers who head to the Cuyahoga Valley National Recreation Area, a 33,000-acre national park area north of Akron. They come for the natural beauty, the miles of smooth Ohio and Erie Canal Towpath Trail to bike or hike, the many activities (including a lively folk music festival in June), and the Cuyahoga Valley Line Railroad passenger train, which makes a ninety-minute, 52-mile trip through the scenic park with stops at Hale Farm and Village or downtown Akron.

The park is a pleasure year-round. Warm-weather visitors can opt to giddyup along the trails, explore rock ledges and caves, or swim in one of the many lakes. In winter, ice skating, cross-country skiing, sledding, and snowshoeing provide frosty fun. Downhill devotees head to the Boston Mills Ski Resort for wintry fun on seven slopes, six chairlifts, and two surface tows; and Brandywine Ski Resort, with one triple lift, four quad lifts, three handle tows, and a vertical drop of 250 feet. For more information on either resort, call (440) 657–2334. Waterfall enthusiasts have two to choose from: breathtaking Brandywine and the smaller Blue Hen Falls, with a quiet woodland setting.

The recreation area is also home to a visitor center housed in a canal-era building (now a canal history museum) that once served as a home, a general store, a tavern, a hotel, and a dance hall. Canal lock demonstrations are conducted on weekends by Park Service staff and volunteers wearing period costumes.

Cuyahoga Valley Line Railroad
Excursions, rates, and times vary; for more details contact the railroad at (800) 468–4070 or (330) 657–2000.

All aboard! Your family will experience the clickety-clack on the tracks and the romance of the rails firsthand with a trip on this scenic railroad. From river floodplain and steep-cut valley walls to ancient stands of evergreen, you'll sit back and relax as the train journeys through historic sites and unspoiled natural areas. Grab a snack or a cool drink in the concession car, and pick up a memento for your favorite railroad buff at the onboard shop. Consider the fall-color train excursion offered in October for a ninety-minute feast for the eyes through some of the state's most beautiful scenery.

For More Information

Peninsula Area Chamber of Commerce, (419) 798–9777.

Amish Country

Tired of faxes and the fast track? Pack up the gang, turn back the clock, and escape to a simpler way of life, Ohio style. The pressures of modern life fade away quickly when you're visiting Amish Country.

Northeast Ohio is the home of the largest population of Amish in the world. About 35,000 of these "plain people" live in a settlement about an hour south of Cleveland that covers several counties, including Holmes, Wayne, Tuscarawas, and

Stark. The gentle and deeply religious Amish culture shuns twenty-first-century technology and comforts, choosing instead a simpler, more rural way of life. Things are made or grown by hand, resulting in unparalleled craftsmanship.

There's plenty for families to see and do in this part of the state. For starters, take a ride on the Ohio Central Railroad in Sugarcreek. The one-hour train ride sputters along behind a steam locomotive at a leisurely 15 miles per hour and takes you through the north-central farmlands that are home to this peaceful people. If you're curious about the Amish way of life, take in the Mennonite Information Center near Berlin, which offers a video introduction to Amish Country, and the Behalt Cyclorama, a 265-foot mural that traces Amish and Mennonite heritage back to the 1500s in Switzerland.

For a closer look at an Amish household, stop at Yoder's Amish Home in Walnut Creek. This now-unoccupied showcase/museum on a 116-acre working farm has two homes and a barn. The first home is typical of an Amish household in the late 1800s, with bare wooden floors and simple furniture. The second is a more "modern" Amish home, with gas floor lamps and running water. The farm's buggy ride is a favorite of young visitors. A 220-seat restaurant was added in 1994. Another option is Schrock's Amish Farm in Berlin (330–893–2951), which offers guided tours, a slide show, and home-baked, farm-made goodies daily. Buggy rides are offered, too. Schrock's is a good spot for a picnic.

As famous as the Amish are for their handcrafts, they're just as renowned for their food. Watch Alfred Guggisberg's famous baby Swiss cheese being prepared—up to 2,500 wheels of cheese are made each day—in a Swiss chalet–style building north of Charm. Don't forget to pick up some of the "holey" goods to take home. Across the road, enjoy old-fashioned Wiener schnitzel, bratwurst, and fresh-baked pies and cakes while being serenaded by accordion players and yodelers at the Chalet in the Valley Restaurant.

Other places to get some wholesome vittles include the Homestead in Charm, with daily specials and a nationally recognized peanut butter pie, and Der Dutchman of Walnut Creek, the first Amish-style restaurant. It opened with just seventy-five seats in 1967 and now serves up to 3,500 meals on a busy day. Specialties include family-style dinners of preservative-free, pan-fried chicken, ham, and roast beef served with homemade bread. After eating, relax on the deck overlooking the valley or sit a spell in an old-fashioned rocker on the front porch.

And, in this part of Ohio, even fast food gets an Amish twist—the McDonald's in Millersburg has a drive-through window reserved just for buggies.

Schrock's Real Amish Experiences

www.realamishexperiences.com.

Want a real Amish experience? Schrock's Real Amish Experiences is happy to oblige. This family-focused business is located in northeast Holmes County, home to the world's largest Amish population.

The Amish Ways of Education

While driving through Amish Country, you'll see a number of one-room schools. The East Holmes School District alone has more than fifty one-room schools, along with five public Amish schools. Your school-age kids will be fascinated by the differences between the Amish schools and their schools back home.

Here's how it works: Amish families can choose to send their children to a one-room school with other Amish children and an Amish teacher or to the public schools, where the students are Amish but the teachers are non-Amish and college educated. In the public school, students may receive a better education but are also exposed to the outside world. Amish schools are not open to travelers, and children walk to and from school, so be careful on the roads.

A variety of activities and special events are offered throughout the year. Schrock's is also home of Schrock's Amish Farm in Berlin, where you'll find a farm filled with animals, old-fashioned fun, and more.

For more information, visit their Web site.

For More Information

Berlin Area Visitors Bureau, (330) 893–3467; www.neohiotravel.com.

Holmes County Chamber of Commerce, (330) 674–3975.

Tuscarawas County Convention and Visitors Bureau, (330) 364–5453.

Wayne County Visitors and Convention Bureau, (330) 264–1800.

Travel Cleveland, www.travelcleveland.com.

Brunswick

Mapleside Farms (all ages) 🍽️ 🏠
294 Pearl Road; (330) 225–5576; www.mapleside.com. Free.

Autumn wouldn't be autumn without a visit to a U-pick farm and apple orchard. One of the best in the area is Mapleside Farms. This 4,000-tree apple orchard surrounds the 300-seat Apple Farm restaurant, apple house, bakery, gift house, and ice-cream parlor.

Bath

Hale Farm and Village (all ages) 🏛️ 🏚️

2686 Oak Hill Road; (877) HALE–FARM, (330) 666–3711; www.wrhs.org. Open from May through October, 11:00 A.M. to 5:00 P.M. Wednesday through Saturday and noon to 5:00 P.M. Sunday. Special programs only November through March. Adults $$$, seniors and children ages three to twelve $$.

Are the Laura Ingalls Wilder books, including *Little House on the Prairie,* popular with your kids? If so, they won't want to miss Hale Farm and Village, located just north of Akron.

The smell of fresh bread baking draws visitors into the village. Once inside, families are treated to a rare view of life in northeastern Ohio's early days. Here the sound of the blacksmith's hammer hitting hot metal, the sight of a sawmill busily cutting wood, and the smell of hearty stew cooking over an open fire take you back to the days when, before sweeping up, you also had to make the broom.

Twenty-one buildings bring the mid-1800s to life. The farm and village are set in the time when Jonathan Hale and his family first arrived in the wilderness of the Western Reserve. Think life is hard in the twenty-first century? Your kids will never complain about their chores again after learning about the workload shared by even the youngest family members of these brave early settlers.

Hale Farm is also the site of popular special events, including Family Day on the Farm, held annually in June; a Children's Day in July, where kids can participate in

Ohio's Hall of Fame Corridor

The area from Cleveland to Canton along Interstate 77 in northeast Ohio has so many halls of fame that it's been dubbed "Ohio's Hall of Fame Corridor." Here you can rock around the clock, check out Super Bowl replays, or learn about Ohio's many inventors. Don't miss these great halls of fame:

- National Inventors Hall of Fame (Akron)
- Pro Football Hall of Fame (Canton)
- Polka Hall of Fame (Cleveland)
- Rock and Roll Hall of Fame (Cleveland)
- Ohio Women's Hall of Fame (Columbus)
- Senior Citizens' Hall of Fame (Columbus)
- Athletic Hall of Fame (Oxford)
- Trapshooting Hall of Fame and Museum (Vandalia)

nineteenth-century games and chores, including whitewashing picket fences and running in a sack race; and Family Days in August. For a special treat, sign up for Breakfast with the Toymaker or the Hale Holiday Brunch held in November and December. Other yearly activities include a rollicking Scottish fest, a popular Civil War encampment, and the autumn Hale Harvest Festival.

After a tour, stop in the well-stocked museum shop, where you'll find samples of handcrafted items made at the farm, including handblown glass, brooms, candles, and blacksmithing and woodworking items.

Akron

Founded in 1825 and closely tied to the building of the Ohio Canal, Akron was once the center of a vast global rubber empire. Today the city remains best known as the corporate home to influential companies such as Goodyear and Uniroyal-Goodrich. The city is so closely identified with the beginnings and growth of the rubber industry that it has gained the nickname "Rubber City." A bit of Akron trivia: The original space suits worn by U.S. astronauts were made and fitted at B. F. Goodrich.

Despite its role as a technological leader, Akron respects its past, with plenty to keep history buffs of all ages busy. Here you'll find one of the most ornate residences in the state, as well as one of the few hotels and shopping centers built in a former silo.

Crowne Plaza Quaker Square (all ages) 🚫 🍴

120 South Broadway Street, Quaker Square; (330) 253–5970; www.quakersquare.com.

Ever sleep in a round room? You and your family will get the chance at the Crowne Plaza Quaker Square, part of the historic Quaker Square complex. The hotel's 196 rooms are perfectly round and contain 450 square feet of space—50 percent more than the average hotel room. There are also 1,000-quare-foot suites. The rooms were converted from the massive Quaker Oats silos that once housed more than 1.5 million bushels of grain and are 120 feet tall and 24 feet in diameter.

Akron is known as the home of the breakfast-cereal industry. It was here in 1854 that Ferdinand Schumacher began selling his homemade oatmeal, later founding Quaker Oats and becoming the undisputed "Oatmeal King of America." Not surprisingly, the once-white silos have been repainted "oatmeal," in honor of their beginnings.

Adjacent Quaker Square Mall and Entertainment Complex is one of the most unusual shopping centers in the country. Located in the heart of downtown Akron, it, too, was carved from the original 1800s Quaker Oats cereal mill. Today it houses thirty shops (kids love My Little Red Wagon, the Quaker Train Shop, and the oatmeal cookies at the Mill St. Candy Co., all on the second floor) as well as restaurants and entertainment facilities. Tasty family fare is available at the popular Depot Restaurant, once the home of Akron's Railway Express Agency terminal. On weekends you can enjoy pasta, pizza, and hobo chicken here surrounded by real railroad cars, locomotives, and one of the world's largest model train displays. Tiny train buffs are encouraged to climb on the great locomotive by the entrance.

Akron Civic Theatre (ages 6 and up) 🎵

182 South Main Street; (330) 253–2488. Free performance first Friday of the month from 11:30 A.M. to 1:00 P.M. Many plays for children. Prices vary.

The Akron Civic Theatre, with its opulent design and ceiling with blinking stars and floating clouds, is one of the few remaining "atmospheric" theaters left in the country. It was lavishly designed by Viennese architect John Eberson to resemble a night in a Moorish garden and recently celebrated its seventy-fifth anniversary.

Invent Now (ages 4 and up) 🖐

221 South Broadway; (800) 968–4332, (330) 762–4433; www.invent.org. Open Monday through Saturday from 9:00 A.M. to 5:00 P.M. and Sunday from noon to 5:00 P.M. $$, families $$$$.

Quick quiz time: What did Thomas Edison, Alexander Graham Bell, and Johann Gutenberg invent?

Don't know the answers? Then run, don't walk, to Invent Now, one of Akron's newest attractions. This dramatic contemporary building in downtown Akron pays homage to the great men and women who, through the ages, revolutionized the world with their inventions. It's a magical place where potatoes are clocks and eggs can fly. It's a place where you can pluck the sky or take off in a bathtub. It's a place where fun comes first and ideas come fast.

Also home to the National Inventors Hall of Fame, it pays homage to the spirit of scientific creativity. Colorful, hands-on exhibits, displays, and workshops are designed to help visitors appreciate how great thinkers have contributed to the American way of life and to inspire you and your children to appreciate, reward, and pursue creativity and invention.

More than 325,000 would-be inventors flock to this 77,000-square-foot facility per year, designed by internationally known architect James Stewart Polshek. It features 29,000 square feet of exhibit space and a wide variety of programs and activities. A special 20,000-square-foot exhibit and inventors workshop area lets you and your children be the inventors: Learn to animate your own cartoon using a computer or create your own laser show. You also can pilot a helicopter (inside the building, of course) and build your own sound system.

Afterward, wander along the building's centerpiece—the soaring, stainless-steel sail that houses five tiers of National Inventors Hall of Fame exhibits, which feature some of the nation's greatest inventors and their inventions. Although big names such as Edison, Ford, and Bell grab center stage, there are also tributes to lesser-known but no less important inventors.

Make Tracks to **Ohio's Ski Resorts**

Skiing in Ohio? Sure. The Buckeye State is home to a number of places that offer the delights of downhill and the thrill of cross-country. Spicy Run is the site of the longest vertical run in the Midwest. Ski areas include:

- **Ohio's Cuyahoga Valley/Brandywine:** 1146 West Highland Road, Sagamore Hills; and Boston Mills, 7100 Riverview Road, Peninsula; (800) 875–4241 for both places

- **Alpine Valley Ski Area,** 10620 Mayfield Road, Chesterland; (440) 285–2211

- **Snow Trails Ski Resort,** 3100 Possum Run Road, Mansfield; (800) 332–7669

- **Clear Fork Ski Area,** 341 Resort Road, Butler; (419) 883–2000

- **Spicy Run Mountain,** P.O. Box 99, Latham 45646; (740) 493–8888

- **Mad River Mountain,** 1000 Snow Valley Road, Zanesfield; (800) 231–7669

Stan Hywet Hall and Gardens (ages 5 and up) 🏛️ 🍁

714 North Portage Path; (330) 836–5533; www.stanhywet.org. Grounds open daily from 9:00 A.M. to 6:00 P.M.; museum and house 10:00 A.M. to 4:30 P.M. April through January; hours vary in winter. Adults $$$, children ages six to twelve $$, children under six free.

One of the city's earliest inventors is honored at the Stan Hywet Hall and Gardens. If you're curious about how Ohio's "other half" lived, you'll find the answers at the state's largest private residence, once home to Frank A. Seiberling, cofounder of Akron's Goodyear Tire & Rubber. Built in 1915, the mansion is considered the finest example of Tudor Revival architecture in the United States. The seventy-acre grounds are most colorful from early May through October. A one-hour tour visits thirty-two rooms.

For forty years the Seiberling family entertained community leaders and heads of state in this sixty-five-room home. Recalling an English country manor, the mansion features lush architectural features, richly carved paneling, molded plaster ceilings, and luminous stained-glass windows. It's surrounded by seventy acres of beautifully landscaped lawns and gardens, as well as a carriage house, greenhouse, and conservatory. Special events geared to families include the Decorated Egg Show held in April and the Christmas holidays, when the house is lavishly decorated inside and out.

All-American **Soap Box Derby**

It has been called "The Greatest Amateur Racing Event in the World," but to the more than one million youngsters who have participated since the 1930s, it's just plain old-fashioned fun. One of Akron's most thrilling events to participate in or just watch is the annual All-American Soap Box Derby, which has been held at the city's Derby Downs each August since 1934. Local champs from all over the world (both boys and girls) ages nine through sixteen compete in gravity-propelled cars in a weeklong celebration.

The idea grew out of the photographic assignment of Dayton, Ohio, newsman Myron Scott, who covered a race of boy-built cars in his home community. He was so impressed that he acquired a copyright for the idea and began development of a similar program on a national scale. The goals of the derby remain the same as they were when it was founded: to teach youngsters basic skills of workmanship, to foster the spirit of competition, and to encourage the perseverance necessary to see a project through to completion.

The first All-American race was held in Dayton in 1934; it moved to Akron the next year for the central location and hilly terrain. Each year since (with the exception of World War II), youngsters from all over have made the pilgrimage to Akron with the racers they have built and driven to victory in their hometowns.

Three racing divisions keep the action lively: The stock division is for first-time builders; the kit-car division offers a more advanced model for more experienced participants; and the master's division features older entrants and encourages creativity and design skills. The week's festivities culminate in Race Day, when young drivers compete for scholarships and prizes.

For more information write P.O. Box 7233, Akron 44306, call (330) 733–8723, or log onto www.aasbd.org.

Goodyear World of Rubber (ages 5 and up) 🔖

1201 East Market Street; (330) 796–7117. Open Monday through Friday from 8:00 A.M. to 4:30 P.M. Free.

If the Stan Hywet house piqued your curiosity about rubber and its impact on Ohio's history and economy, stop at the Goodyear World of Rubber museum on Akron's east side to learn more about this revolutionary invention. The museum is on the fourth floor of Goodyear Hall, part of the company's headquarters complex on East Market Street.

Ever wonder how rubber is made? Wander through the exhibits on your own or take a guided tour, and you'll learn as the museum traces the material's beginnings from Charles Goodyear's kitchen laboratory and follows the growth of his company, founded in 1898. The fascinating Charles Goodyear Memorial Collection outlines the discovery of the vulcanization process that made rubber a practical material for many uses. The collection was exhibited for several years at the Smithsonian Institution before it was moved to Akron.

Other highlights include a simulated rubber plantation, Indianapolis 500 cars, an artificial heart, a history of blimps and other light aircraft, and exhibits that show how tires are made.

Akron Zoo (all ages)

500 Edgewood Avenue; (937) 375–2550; www.akronzoo.com. Open year-round, Monday through Sunday May through October from 10:00 A.M. to 5:00 P.M.; November through April from 11:00 A.M. to 4:00 P.M. Adults $$, children ages two to fourteen $.

When Columbus set foot in the Americas, he was greeted by animals and birds unlike any seen in Europe or Africa. This "New World" animal kingdom is featured at the Akron Zoo, located on Edgewood Avenue west of downtown.

Some zoos are overwhelming, offering more than a family can possibly squeeze into one day. Not so the Akron Zoo, which is manageable in an afternoon and perfect for preschoolers' short attention spans. The park, which celebrated its fiftieth anniversary in 2003, features animals found in North and South America in a scenic, naturally wooded area. Highlights include Tiger Valley, Penguin Point, and Ohio Farmland. Tiger Valley is an interactive adventure filled with Sumatran tigers, sun bears, and flamingos, as well as a train, conservation area, and tree house.

Discover what the early explorers may have seen on their historic travels: bighorn sheep, bobcats, reptiles, jaguars, prairie dogs, porcupines, and the massive black bear. Many of these animals once roamed the areas that are now your backyard. Watch river otters cavort in a pool in an underwater viewing area; take a ride on a pony; feed cows, goats, and other farm animals in the Ohio Farmyard; or learn about endangered species and what your family can do to aid in their preservation.

In 2005 the museum opened its largest expansion ever, the Legends of the Wild. With sixteen new exhibits, twenty different species, and more than 380 animals, it's a can't-miss stop. Where else can you learn that Andean condors were believed to bring up the sun and the Mayan myth of how the jaguar got its spots? The storytellers ring is a family favorite. Also new in 2005 was Komodo Kingdom, featuring Komodo dragons, Galapagos tortoises, and Chinese alligators.

Carousel Dinner Theatre (ages 5 and up, depending on performance)
🎵 🍽️
1275 East Waterloo Road; (800) 362–4100; www.carouseldinnertheatre.com.

A popular spot for families, the Carousel Dinner Theatre is America's largest professional dinner theater, and it is open year-round. Rising stars and established talents are featured in Broadway's best musicals, including *The Unsinkable Molly Brown, Nunsense II, The Will Rogers Follies,* and *Guys and Dolls.* In 2006 shows will include *Footloose, Grease, Singin' in the Rain,* and *The Buddy Holly Story.*

Where to Eat

Lou & Hy's Deli, 1949 West Market Street; (330) 836–9159. New York–style deli known for its chicken soup, kosher sandwiches, and delicious desserts. $

Michael Trecaso's Restaurant, 780 West Market Street; (330) 253–7751. Casual family-style dining with Italian specialties and a smoke-free dining room. $–$$

Trackside Grille, Quaker Square; (330) 253–5970. The best bet for families with young kids, with a great Sunday brunch, clowns, trains, and an extensive kids' menu. $–$$

Where to Stay

Crowne Plaza Quaker Square, Quaker Square; (330) 253–5970. Where else can you stay in former oat silos? With 176 rooms and ten two-bedroom suites, some quite large due to the unusual spaces, there's plenty to choose from. There are also adjacent shopping, four theme restaurants, a model-railroad museum, and more. Listed on the National Register of Historic Places. $$–$$$

Fairfield Inn, 70 Rothrock Road; (330) 668–2700, (800) 228–2800. Bright, comfortable rooms; genuine heartland hospitality; and a complimentary continental breakfast bar make this a good budget bet. $

Holiday Inn Express, 2940 Chenoweth Road; (330) 644–7126, (800) HOLIDAY (465–5629). Handily located, with 129 rooms, an outdoor pool, a restaurant, and packages to nearby Geauga Lake & Wildwater Kingdom. $$

For More Information

Akron/Summit County Convention & Visitors Bureau, 77 East Mill Street, Akron 44308; (800) 245–4254; www.visit akron-summit.org.

North Canton/Canton

Pro Football Hall of Fame (ages 4 and up) 🏈

2121 George Halas Drive Northwest; (330) 456–8207, (888) 388–FAME (3263); www
.profootballhof.com. Open daily from 9:00 A.M. to 8:00 P.M. in summer; closes at 5:00
P.M. the rest of the year. Adults $$, children ages fourteen and younger $, family
groups $$$$.

One . . . two . . . three . . . hike! If football is your game of choice, rush over to the Pro
Football Hall of Fame for an insightful view of one of America's most popular sports.
Canton was chosen as the hall's site because the National Football League was
founded here in 1920.

Included in the modern, 83,000-square-foot, four-building complex are four
eye-catching exhibition areas, a football action movie theater, a research library, a
snack bar, and a bustling museum store that sells licensed items from all of the
NFL's teams. Twin enshrinement halls permanently honor the greats of pro football,
including 203 inductees from 1892 to modern times. The Hall of Fame opened in
1963 and recently celebrated its fortieth anniversary.

A 7-foot bronze statue of Jim Thorpe, the legendary hero of early-day pro foot-
ball, greets visitors. Nearby, the Exhibition Rotunda tells the story of the sport's
beginnings and includes priceless souvenirs and mementos of the early days. A 52-
foot dome in the shape of (what else?) a football holds the Professional Football
Today display, with representatives from each of the current NFL teams. Newly
acquired items include the shoes and gloves worn by Cadillac Williams of the Tampa
Bay Buccaneers when he set a new rookie rushing record. A new exhibit honors the
New England Patriots winning streak.

Also worth a gander is the art gallery, with winning, action-packed photos; the
Leagues and Champions Room, where AFL and NFL histories are recounted and
the Super Bowl series is chronicled in colorful detail; and the moving Black Man in
Pro Football, which honors early African-American players. The museum is also site
of the weeklong Pro Football Hall of Fame Festival in July, in which football's greatest
names meet in Canton for an exciting array of activities that include a balloon classic
invitation, food fest and fireworks, a ribs burn-off, drum corps competition, Kickoff
Sunday, induction of the newest enshrinees, and, of course, a rousing game at
Fawcett Stadium.

McKinley Presidential Library and Museum (ages 3 and up) 🏈

800 McKinley Monument Drive Northwest; (330) 455–7043. Open Monday through
Saturday from 9:00 A.M. to 5:00 P.M. and Sunday from noon to 5:00 P.M. Museum admis-
sion: adults $$, children ages three to eighteen $, families $$$. Monument admission
is free.

Canton is also home to the three-part McKinley Complex, including a National Memorial, a Museum of History and Industry, and Discover World. All honor our nation's twenty-fifth president, William McKinley (1843–1901), originally from Canton.

The memorial is a double-domed structure, sheathed with pink granite from Massachusetts. Inside the memorial are the remains of President and Mrs. McKinley, as well as their daughters Katie and Ida, who died of diphtheria as children.

Happier memories are found in the Museum of History, which recounts some 200 years of American history. Future homemakers imagine preparing a meal in the authentic pioneer kitchen; kids of all ages love the collection of historic toys that spotlight children's precious possessions before the days of Nintendo and television. Another section includes tangible remembrances of William McKinley: the clothing he wore, the furniture he used, and personal and political mementos that represent his life as a public and private figure. Other popular displays include the vintage "Street of Shops" and the operating HO gauge model-train complex, which represents the Pennsylvania Railroad tracks through nearby Ohio towns such as Orrville, Massillon, Canton, Louisville, Alliance, and Sebring.

Also located here are the Museum of Industry and a starstruck planetarium. Kids, however, favor Discover World, an adjacent science center. From the minute you're greeted by the spine-tingling roar of a life-size allosaurus (it moves its legs and opens its jaws thanks to the magic of robotics) at the entrance, you know you're not in another stuffy museum.

Wander inside and you'll find yourself in a landscape that reveals exciting secrets of many years ago. Explore the kinds of creatures that roamed Earth as you examine fossil remains and walk in the shadow of a massive mastodon's skeleton. Peek inside the circular tent of a long-vanished Native American tribe, where dioramas show how Stark County prehistoric Native Americans might have lived. Farther along, you'll hear the trickle of water and the sound of birds as you pass through our present-day ecosystem and approach humankind's exploration of the next great frontier—outer space.

Once aboard Space Station Earth, you'll learn how lasers and light waves behave and the way air reacts under pressure. Pretend you're a TV meteorologist and examine weather conditions in Ohio as well as around the world. Discover World encourages children to explore the past, present, and future.

Hoover Historical Center (ages 5 and up)

1875 Easton Street; (330) 499–0287. Hours are 1:00 to 5:00 P.M. Tuesday through Sunday. Free.

Remember your mother's old upright vacuum cleaner? Chances are you'll find it in the Hoover Historical Center, a rich repository of carpet-cleaning history. A large, Victorian farmhouse built in 1853 houses memorabilia that traces the growth of the Hoover Company through artifacts, pictures, and, of course, products. Here you'll find not only your mother's but your grandmother's vacuum, unsuccessful preelectric carpet cleaners, and more. The home was originally the home of W. H. "Boss" Hoover, a north Canton entrepreneur who bought the patent for the first commercially successful portable vacuum from inventor Murray Spangler. The center is now owned and administered by Walsh University. If you're lucky, you'll be treated to a game of old-fashioned baseball by the 1860s-era Hoover Sweepers, a team sponsored by the center. There are also herb gardens and a gift shop. The museum was reopened in 1999 to coincide with the company's ninetieth anniversary.

Harry London Candies (ages 4 and up)

5353 Lauby Road; (330) 494–0833; www.londoncandies.com. Open Monday through Saturday from 9:00 A.M. to 4:00 P.M. Tours ($) are given daily on the half hour; reservations are required.

More than 500 varieties of chocolate and gourmet candies have been made here since 1922. You can watch the process on forty-five-minute guided tours that provide insight into candy making and the history of these sweet treats. Besides the chance to taste the final products, the highlight for most families is the Chocolate Hall of Fame, which details candy making through history.

Canton Classic Car Museum (ages 5 and up)

555 Market Avenue South, Canton; (330) 455–3603; www.cantonclassiccar.org. Open daily from 10:00 A.M. to 5:00 P.M. $; free for children under six.

More than forty-five models dating from 1904 to 1981 star in this museum, which also features other antiques, vintage toys, and political items. A highlight is the 1937 Studebaker "Bandit Car," originally purchased by the Canton Police Department to retaliate against mobsters. Older boys love the gun ports in the windows, bulletproof tires, and trunk and rear-seat arsenals.

Where to Eat

Bender's Tavern, 137 Court Street Southwest; (330) 453–8424. Turn-of-the-twentieth-century tavern and hotel is a local favorite, with a children's menu and a wide variety of entrees. $–$$

The Stables, 2317 Thirteenth Street; (330) 452–1230. Horse lover? Football fan? Satisfy both in this converted horse barn decorated with football memorabilia. Casual atmosphere and nice kids' menu. $–$$

Where to Stay

Best Suites of America, 4914 Everhard Road; (330) 499–1011, (800) 237–8466. This well-run suite hotel has 102 rooms, complimentary evening beverages, free breakfast, a coin laundry, refrigerators and comfy recliners in all rooms. There's also a pool, a must for kids. $$

Comfort Inn, 5345 Broadmoor Circle Northwest; (330) 492–1331, (800) 221–2222. Situated in a quiet location, this 124-room hotel has free movies, a pool with a sundeck, and a free deluxe breakfast buffet. $–$$

Fairfield Inn, 5335 Broadmoor; (330) 493–7373, (800) 228–2800. Handy budget hotel with sixty-two rooms and a small, heated indoor pool and whirlpool. $

For More Information

Canton/Stark County Convention & Visitors Bureau, 229 Wells Avenue Northwest, Canton 44703-2642; (800) 533–4302; www.cantonchamber.org.

Bolivar/Zoar

Fort Laurens State Memorial and Museum (ages 5 and up)

Interstate 77 and Highway 212; (330) 874–2059, (800) 238–8914; www.ohiohistory.org. **Hours vary; closed Monday and Tuesday and from September through May. Museum admission: $, free for children under six.**

Few think Ohio—a long way from the battlefields and cities of the East Coast—played a part in the American Revolution. The eighty-one-acre Fort Laurens was the only American fort built in Ohio during the Revolutionary War. Today it's the home of many lively military reenactments and provides the kind of history lesson your children won't mind learning.

The fort traces the lives of the 176 men and 5 women who lived here more than two centuries ago. They had been sent to the Ohio country to neutralize the Indian threat and establish a western supply post for an eventual attack on British Detroit to the north. The fort was christened for Henry Laurens, then president of the Continental Congress. After a long and bitter American occupation, the fort was abandoned in 1779 when hopes of attacking Detroit were given up.

A good overview of the site's history and an intriguing collection of artifacts found on archaeological digs are featured in the museum, which now sits on what was once the fort's west gate. Lifelike mannequins wearing uniforms of the period, weapons, and household goods help tell the fort's story, as does an informative, action-packed video.

Just outside the museum, the Tomb of the Unknown Patriot pays homage to the courage and perseverance of those who once lived at Fort Laurens and fought and died for American independence. A shallow trench that surrounds a part of the museum outlines the shape of the original fort. Also surrounding the museum is a large park—including a restful picnic area—where reenactments are held.

Zoar Village (ages 4 and up) 🏛

198 Main Street, Zoar; (330) 874–3011 or (800) 262–6195; www.ohiohistory.org/places/
zoar. Hours vary with the season; closed October through April. Adults $$, children
ages six to twelve $, free for children under six.

Not far from the fort is another remnant of the state's past. Zoar Village was settled
in 1817 by a group of pioneers seeking religious freedom. A group of 300 German
Separatists—so named because they had broken with the established Lutheran
Church—left Germany and founded on the Ohio plains one of the most notable
experiments in communal living in our country's history.

Life at Zoar, which means "sanctuary from evil," was far from heavenly, however.
Because food was scarce and work difficult to find, a communal style of living was
adopted. Ahead of their time, the German Separatists believed in equality for men
and women. The village grew and crops flourished, with a flour mill, planing mill, and
woolen mill soon springing up. By the mid-1830s Zoar was self-sustaining, and the vil-
lagers had become known throughout the state for their skill in gardening.

Today this quiet village offers a respite from the confusions of modern life. Many of
the public buildings have been restored and welcome families curious about this
bygone era.

Your first stop should be the former Zoar Store, built in 1833. Once the center of
the community and the area's post office, it sold products produced in and outside
the village. Today it's where you'll pick up your tour tickets and reproduction nine-
teenth-century wares, as well as view an informative video on the village.

Don't miss the impressive two-story, Georgian-style Number One House, once the
home of Zoar leader Joseph Baumeler. The home features fine examples of Zoar fur-
niture and crafts. Not far away is the Garden and Greenhouse, built in 1835. The for-
mal gardens throughout the village square were designed in a geometric plan based
on the Bible; during their time, the villagers became known for their skill in design.
Other popular stops include the 1825 Tinshop, the 1834 Blacksmith Shop (with its
great charcoal-fired forge and its huge bellows), the 1840 Wagon Shop, and the 1841
Dairy (the workers lived on the second floor). Finally, follow your nose to the 1845
Bakery, where Zoar members used to come once a day to receive, free of charge, as
much bread as they needed. Today demonstrations of the bakery's ovens turn out
fragrant bread, pretzels, and gingerbread.

Where to Eat

Zoar Tavern & Inn, 162 Main Street;
(330) 874–2170. Located in the center of
town, this historic tavern was once home
to the town's doctor. It features fresh
seafood, steaks, burgers, and a kids'
menu. Try the famous bread pudding. $$

Massillon

Massillon Museum (all ages) 🌀

121 Lincoln Way East; (330) 833–4061; www.massillonmuseum.org. Open Tuesday through Saturday from 9:30 A.M. to 5:00 P.M. and Sunday from noon to 5:00 P.M. **Free.**

It's worth a drive out of the way to stop at this tucked-away treasure off the historic Lincoln Highway. Behind the facade of this former 1930s Art Deco dry goods store are more than 100,000 works representing both local and Native American history. Textiles, photography, and Ohio-made glass are featured, but kids especially like the Immel Circus display, a 100-square-foot hand-carved replica of a circus, with a staggering 2,620 pieces.

Ohio Society of Military History (all ages)

316 Lincoln Way East; (330) 832–5553. Open Tuesday through Friday 10:00 A.M. to 5:00 P.M.; Saturday 10:00 A.M. to 3:00 P.M. **Free.**

Close to the Massillon Museum is the small Ohio Society of Military History, which features medals, photographs, and a fascinating Civil War collection.

New Philadelphia

Founded in the early 1800s, today's New Philadelphia is a light industrial center and a popular vacation spot, thanks mostly to the nearby recreational opportunities in the 16,000-acre Muskingum Conservancy District.

Schoenbrunn Village State Memorial (ages 4 and up) 🏛 🛝

Highway 259 (East High Avenue); (330) 339–3636, (800) 752–2711; www.ohiohistory .org/places/schoenbr. Open Wednesday through Saturday from 9:30 A.M. to 5:00 P.M. and Sunday from noon to 5:00 P.M. May through September only; closed the rest of the year. Adults $$, children ages six to twelve $, **free** for children under six.

In 1772 Schoenbrunn Village was settled by Moravian missionaries in an attempt to convert the local Delaware Indians to Christianity. It was here that the state's first schoolhouse was built to educate the Native American children. Despite the fact that there was no threat to its pacifist beliefs and its acceptance by the local population, Schoenbrunn was abandoned in 1777 because of the advance of the British and the impending Revolutionary War.

Today the village, whose name means "beautiful spring," has been restored to appear as it did more than 200 years ago. There are seventeen reconstructed log buildings, the original mission cemetery, and two and one-half acres of planted fields. Costumed volunteers in eighteenth-century attire help bring the village to life, re-creating a fascinating and fateful time in Ohio history.

For a quick overview of the area, stop by the small museum near the village. Afterward, wander among the reconstructed buildings, which include a simple meetinghouse, the schoolhouse, a recently renovated visitor orientation center (which tells how the area's log cabins were made), and other buildings.

Where to Eat

Dante's Pizza and Pasta, 261 West High Street; (330) 339–4444. Elegant rooms with a casual atmosphere help this classic Italian eatery stand out. Most things are made on the premises, including delectable pastas and sauces. $$

Randall's, 1013 Front Avenue Southwest; (330) 339–7667. A local favorite with informal family dining accented by Amish and American country-style decor. The Amish-made pies are famous. Children's menu. $

Where to Stay

Holiday Inn, 131 Bluebell Drive Southwest; (330) 339–7731. Well-run chain hotel with 108 rooms, sauna, two pools, restaurant, and free in-room movies. $–$$

Schoenbrunn Inn and Suites by Christopher, 1186 West High Avenue; (330) 339–4334; www.christopherhotels .com. Located in the heart of Ohio's Amish country, this inn features sixty rooms and suites with Amish-style simplicity and charm, a deluxe complimentary continental breakfast, sauna, hot tub, and more. $–$$

Steubenville

Creegan Company (ages 3 and up)

510 Washington Street; (740) 283–3708; www.creegans.com. Tours Monday through Friday by appointment. **Free.**

Watch It Made in the U.S.A., a guide to companies that make America's favorite products, recently named Steubenville's colorful Creegan Company as one of the best factory tours in the country. It's worth the trip to this tiny town near the West Virginia border.

What makes Creegan so great? It's not so much the tour itself but what the company creates. Creegan is the nation's largest manufacturer of animated and costume characters. Familiar faces include Beary Bear, Plentiful Penguin, Strawberry Bunny, and the Gamuffins, who are seen in retail shops and malls across the country. Creegan also designs characters for Sea World, Hershey's Chocolate World, and Disney World.

Inside a former Montgomery Ward department store at the corner of Washington and Fifth Streets, visitors of all ages watch as Creegan employees bring an array of characters to life. The three-floor factory bustles with activity as artists and craftspeople design, sculpt, decorate, and mechanize hundreds of animated creatures.

After being greeted by Beary Bear, the company's official mascot, a costumed guide leads you through a room that contains what must be thousands of spools of ribbon in every color, pattern, and texture. Puppet heads, scenery, and props battle for space with silk flowers and other craft materials. A large, lifelike white gorilla stands beside three rosy-cheeked elves. Along the way, the tour, which lasts forty-five minutes to an hour, passes through the art, mechanical, carpentry, and sewing departments.

Up a wide staircase is the art shop, where workers make costumes and paint faces on molded plastic heads. On the main floor your kids will watch with fascination as a huge vacuum-form machine presses out the puppet faces and uses white plastic and molds to create various facial expressions.

Downstairs in the main sculpting area, one woman creates all the characters' head molds. Shelves contain hundreds of plaster molds shaped like heads, feet, hands, and animals. Farther along, in the mechanics/electronics department, brave children can peek into some headless mechanized bodies to discover the characters' sophisticated electronic insides and see how the parts come together to produce body movements.

Tours are **free** and include cake, candy, or cookie samples from the company's Fancy Food Department. The on-site Christmas Shop features company-made items such as trees, lights, ornaments, gifts, and decorations. The Grampa Creegan Puppet Shop displays hand and rod puppets and deluxe, plush stuffed animals from around the world.

Where to Stay

Holiday Inn, 1401 University Boulevard; (740) 282–0901. Reasonable rates, 121 rooms with coin laundry, and free in-room movies. $–$$

For More Information

Greater Steubenville Convention and Visitors Bureau, (740) 283–4935.

Jefferson County Chamber of Commerce, (740) 282–6226.

Coshocton

Derived from travelers' spellings of Native American words meaning either "river crossing" or "place of the black bear," this unusually named town on the banks of the Muskingum River was once called Tuscarawa. The legendary Johnny Appleseed planted some of his orchards here, but the town was best known as an important canal port and a thriving milling center from the 1830s through the Civil War. The town honors its heritage during the annual Coshocton Canal Festival and Parade, held each August to commemorate the arrival of the first canal boat, the *Monticello*, which docked at Port Roscoe in 1830.

Roscoe Village (all ages)

381 Hill Street; for information on special events or the village call (800) 877–1830; www.roscoevillage.com. Village admission is **free**; tours are given daily 10:00 A.M. to 3:00 P.M. Tours: Adults $$, children ages five to twelve $, children under five **free.**

A family favorite, Roscoe Village was named one of the twenty best historic restorations in America by *Early American Life* magazine. The original town fell on hard times after the canal closed because of a flood in 1913, but it was reborn in 1968 as a living-history museum, where interpreters and craftspeople bring the nineteenth century to life for thousands of happy visitors.

Start your visit with the wide-screen, multi-image show in the visitor center and then explore the village's seven living-history buildings (including an early-nineteenth-century house, a blacksmith shop, a schoolhouse, and an 1840s canal tollhouse) and nineteen unusual shops. Or take the kids on the *Monticello III*, which offers once-in-a-lifetime, forty-five-minute horse-drawn canal boat rides (fares are $6.00 for adults and $3.00 for kids ages five to twelve). Afterward, snack on goodies from the Village Bakery, sample regional cuisine at the recently renovated 1838 Old Warehouse restaurant, or cool off with homemade ice cream from Captain Nye's Sweet Shop and Cafe.

Many families prefer to visit during one of the annual events, including the rousing Dulcimer Days held each May. The festival features the mid-eastern regional dulcimer championships as well as exhibits, sales, workshops, and performances on an open-air stage. Other popular weekends include Summer Fest, the Old Time Music Fest in September, Apple Butter Stirrin' in October, and the festive Christmas Candlelighting in December.

Where to Stay and Eat

Coshocton Village Inn and Suites, 115 North Water Street; (740) 622–9455. Comfortable and well located with sixty-four rooms and complimentary breakfast. $–$$

Old Warehouse Restaurant, 400 North Whitewoman Street; (740) 622–4001. Restored 1838 building is decorated to look like the inside of a canal boat. Casual dress. $–$$

For More Information

Coshocton County Convention and Visitors Bureau, 101 North Whitewoman Street; (740) 622–4877, (800) 338–4724; www.visitcoshocton.com.

Lucas

Malabar Farm State Park (all ages) 🏛️ 🅰️

4050 Bromfield Road; (419) 892–2784; www.malabarfarm.org. **Hours vary with the season. $.**

This educational farm and thirty-two-room Big House, built by Pulitzer prize–winning Ohio author and conservationist Louis Bromfield, gained notoriety as the wedding site for his friends Humphrey Bogart and Lauren Bacall. Once Bromfield's private home, it's the only working farm in the Ohio state park system. The grounds feature the house, which contains a variety of antiques, art, and rare books; a working farm with wagon rides ($1.00 for adults); and a variety of seasonal special events, including the popular Ohio Heritage Days in late September. Naturalist Mike leads tours of the farm and serves as a guide on the kids' section of the Web site, worth checking out before you go. There's also a farmers' market, wagon rides, 14 miles of backcountry trails, and stocked ponds with **free** fishing poles.

Loudonville

Great Mohican Indian Powwow and Rendezvous (all ages)

(800) 722–7588; www.mohicanreservation.com. **Powwows are held twice yearly, in July and September. Adults $$, children ages six to twelve $.**

Have your kids ever wanted to learn the right way to throw a tomahawk? If so, they'll have a field day during the Great Mohican Indian Powwow and Rendezvous, held twice yearly in Loudonville, in the southern part of the region. Here's their chance to see feather headdresses and war paint firsthand, as well as learn about the intricacies and long-standing traditions of Native American culture.

Don't expect rubber tomahawks. This is a real Native American powwow. Native Americans from tribes such as the Navajo, Cherokee, Lakota, Sioux, Shawnee, Seneca, Iroquois, Comanche, and Ottawa travel from around the country to meet on Mohican Valley territory for fellowship and competition.

Although the Traditional and Fancy Dance competitions are limited to Native Americans, visitors are encouraged to enjoy the event as spectators. Tribes perform as their ancestors did for generations through movements that signify great spiritual meaning for Native Americans. The powwow offers non–Native Americans a rare chance to see this art form firsthand.

This multievent festival also includes Native American foods, storytelling, hoop dancers, herbalists, blacksmiths, and other demonstrations of Native American culture. Some thirty Native American craftspeople, including famous flute maker and player Arnold Richardson, sell their wares, including pottery, beadwork, silver, quillwork, pipestone carvings, wood and bone carvings, leatherwork, baskets, paintings, and music.

Rails to **Trails**

Once a beloved form of transportation, railroads met their match in the 1950s and 1960s as interstate highways, air travel, and inland waterways boomed. In time, tracks were abandoned across the Midwest. In Ohio, many of these trails have been renovated and converted to recreational paths by the Rails-to-Trails Conservancy. Efforts across the state have secured thirty-eight trails, which stretch for more than 300 miles from Cleveland to Columbus, Akron to Zanesville, and everywhere in between. The number of rail-trails in Ohio is expected to continue to grow. For more information contact the state tourism office at (800) BUCKEYE (282–5393) or visit www.railtrails.org for general information.

Mohican State Park (all ages)
3116 Highway 3; (419) 994–5125; www.dnr.state.oh.us/parks. Open daily from 8:00 A.M. to 9:00 P.M. Free.

One of the state's most scenic areas, this 1,110-acre park includes a variety of family-friendly recreational opportunities. At the forest's upper edge is the 113-foot Pleasant Hill Dam, the highest in the Muskingum Conservancy District. Within the park is the Mohican River, popular for swimming and canoeing.

Also located here are a 1,000-foot, 200-feet-deep gorge; a recess cave; waterfalls; a bridge; and plenty of canoeing, hiking, camping, and picnicking. There's also a rustic lodge. Try and visit in the fall, when the drive and the park are especially gorgeous. The best view can be had from the Memorial Shrine and fire tower and Clearfork Gorge. A great 2-mile walk on the Lyons Falls Trail curves through the park. If you're looking for a place to stay, try the ninety-six-room lodge or the twenty-five two-bedroom family cottages that accommodate six.

Materials Park/ASM International (all ages)
9639 Kinsman Road; (440) 338–5151. The building and grounds are open from 8:30 A.M. to 10:00 P.M. daily. No organized tours offered. Free.

Heavy metal. It's a strange sight when it rises from more than forty-five acres of rolling hills. Has a spaceship set down right here in the farmland off Highway 87 some 20 miles east of Cleveland, you wonder?

Nope. The huge geodesic dome, the largest open-face dome in the world, is the headquarters of ASM International and one of the most photographed sites in the state. Created by Cleveland architect John Terence Kelly, it was completed in 1959. One of the most outstanding features of the building is the dome, also known as a "space lattice" designed by R. Buckminster Fuller.

Defined by a network of hexagonal and pentagonal shapes, the openwork dome stands 103 feet high, 250 feet in diameter, and weighs some eighty tons. It's formed of 13 miles of aluminum tubing and tension rods (65,000 parts!). In all, it resembles a giant, round honeycomb.

The dome has become a tourist attraction in itself, but visitors also enjoy the circular mineral garden set beneath the dome in a landscaped area. Educational as well as decorative, it displays more than seventy-five specimens of raw mineral ores, all labeled with identification for miniature rock hounds. A fountain sprays water 30 feet high in the center over the minerals below. A sundial on the other side of the garden accurately reflects the time of day.

Another favorite site is the apple tree grove. When Isaac Newton discovered the law of gravity, the Royal Society of England identified the apple tree he sat under and kept it. Before the tree died, cuttings were taken. One ended up here in 1968. Originally marked and kept in a fenced-in area, it later was moved to a grove of similar-looking trees to protect it.

Youngstown

Butler Institute of American Art (ages 4 and up)
524 Wick Avenue; (330) 743–1711; www.butlerart.com. Open Tuesday, Thursday, Friday, and Saturday from 11:00 A.M. to 4:00 P.M.; Wednesday from 11:00 A.M. to 8:00 P.M.; and Sunday from noon to 4:00 P.M. Free.

American art from the colonial days through modern times provides the focus for this vast permanent collection, the first in the country built solely to house American art. It was founded in 1919 by industrialist Joseph G. Butler Jr.

Highlights include major works by Thomas Eakins, Winslow Homer, Frederic Remington, Andy Warhol, and Mary Cassatt. Changing exhibitions drawn from around the world, a hands-on children's gallery, and a gallery of sports art intrigue families.

Mill Creek Metroparks (all ages)
Glenwood Avenue; (330) 702–3000; www.millcreekmetroparks.com. Open daily from dawn to dusk. Free.

Nature lovers in east-central Ohio rave about this 2,500-acre park. Included are three lakes, Lanterman Falls, a 6-mile-long gorge, and Riverside Gardens—an eleven-acre garden with rose gardens, perennials, shrubs, trees, and more than 25,000 tulips in the spring. Two overlooks provide scenic views of the park and city. Activities include hiking, golf, tennis, fishing, and picnicking.

Also in the park are the Ford Nature Center, a former residence built of stone with three rooms that display live reptiles and hands-on displays and offers weekly nature hikes; and Lanterman's Mill, a restored nineteenth-century, water-powered gristmill that dates to 1845.

Where to Stay and Eat

Comfort Inn, 4055 Belmont Avenue; (330) 759–3180, (800) 228–5150. Conveniently located chain hotel with 144 rooms, heated pool, and **free** continental breakfast. On-site is an authentic Mexican restaurant, the Cancun Cantina, known for its freshly prepared fare. $

Central Ohio

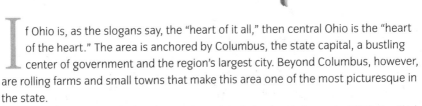

I f Ohio is, as the slogans say, the "heart of it all," then central Ohio is the "heart of the heart." The area is anchored by Columbus, the state capital, a bustling center of government and the region's largest city. Beyond Columbus, however, are rolling farms and small towns that make this area one of the most picturesque in the state.

But central Ohio is not all work and no play. Columbus is home to COSI, the "kid-tested and kid-approved" Center of Science and Industry, where you can ride a high-wire bicycle or step inside a lunar module. It's also home to the groundbreaking Wexner Center for the Arts, known for its mind-bending modern art exhibits. From city streets to country fields and everywhere in between, there's plenty for families to explore.

Khristi's
TopPicks for fun in Central Ohio

1. Center of Science and Industry (COSI) in Columbus

2. German Village in Columbus

3. Columbus Zoo in Powell

4. Olentangy Indian Caverns in Delaware

5. Circleville Pumpkin Festival

CENTRAL OHIO

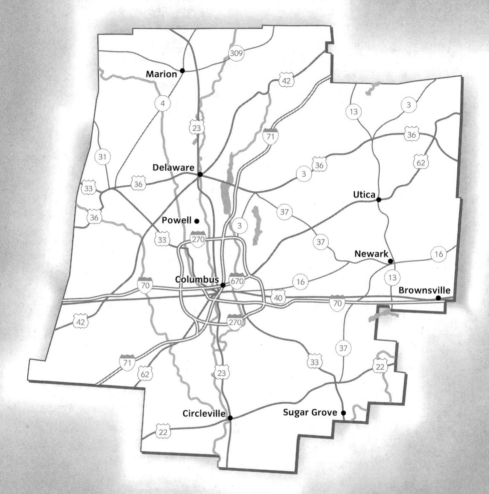

Columbus

Ohio's capital is reinventing itself. Once a sleepy government town, it's now a thriving city—the state's largest and the sixteenth largest in the United States—on the cutting edge of scientific and technological progress. Local author and cartoonist James Thurber once said that "Columbus is a town in which almost anything is likely to happen and in which almost everything has." For families, that translates into an exciting city that knows how to have fun.

This is a city of firsts. The first banana split was made at Foeller's Drug Store in response to a customer request for "something different" and was originally called the "Five-Six-Seven." One of the first American kindergartens was established here in 1938. The first gorilla born in captivity made its debut in 1956 at the Columbus Zoo.

Downtown boasts a wide variety of things to see and do including the original COSI, Center of Science and Industry, which inspired science centers across the country (there's now an outpost in Toledo).

Bicentennial Park (all ages)
Rich Street and Civic Center Drive. Free.

The Scioto River waterfront is home to two of the city's most popular parks. Bicentennial Park is the site of the explosive Red, White & Boom fireworks display held each July. The rest of the summer, it's a serene oasis in the city with beautifully landscaped grounds, a gurgling fountain, well-used bike trails, and the best skyline view in the city.

Santa Maria (all ages)
90 West Broad Street, Battelle Park; (614) 645–8760; www.santamaria.org. Hours vary with the season; call ahead. Closed November through March. $, children under five free.

Battelle Riverfront Park, another great picnic spot, is home to the flag-flying *Santa Maria*, a full-size, carefully crafted replica of Christopher Columbus's flagship. When he set sail in 1492, Columbus was carried by a 98-foot-long wooden ship called a *nao*, or a typical merchant's cargo ship.

More than 500 years later, you can visit one of the world's most authentic representations of Columbus's flagship. Built for the city's 1992 quincentennial celebration of Columbus's landing, the vintage vessel lets would-be sailors experience life on board a historic sailing vessel. Costumed interpreters tell how sailors of yore whiled away long days at sea and often ate cold meals due to fear of galley, or kitchen, fires. You'll also see their on-deck sleeping quarters. Staying in town for a while? Consider booking a pirate-themed party for a birthday your child will long remember.

Ohio Capitol Square Complex (ages 3 and up) 🏛

Broad Street; (614) 728–2695, (614) 752–6350; www.statehouse.state.oh.us/tours/
index.cfm. Open daily from 9:00 A.M. to 7:00 P.M. Guided forty-five-minute tours are
offered Monday through Friday from 9:00 A.M. to 3:00 P.M.; on weekends, a tour guide
is on-site from 11:00 A.M. to 4:00 P.M. Self-guided tours are available daily from 7:00
A.M. to 7:00 P.M. and are free.

Back on land, a good place to get a feel for the pulse of the city—and the state—is
the Ohio Capitol Square Complex on Broad Street. Who needs C-SPAN when you and
your children can watch history in the making during a visit to one of the oldest state-
houses in continuous use in the United States?

First used in 1857, it's affectionately called the "Hat Box Capitol" because of its
distinctive rotunda and is considered to be one of the country's finest examples of
Greek Revival architecture. Ironically, architect Frank Lloyd Wright considered it "the
most honest of state capitols," even though much of it was built by penitentiary
inmates. This majestic structure was built of Columbus limestone after the city
became the state's third capital in 1816. It's one of the few capitols in the country
that doesn't sport a dome, but its ceilings and moldings are decorated with twenty-
four-karat gold leaf. It took six architects twenty-two years to complete it at a cost of
$1,359,121.

After a quick introduction in the ground-floor visitor center, follow in the footsteps of Presidents Garfield and Harding, who both served in the Senate Chamber.
Abraham Lincoln was speaking here in 1861 when he learned that the electoral college had confirmed his presidential victory (the chair he sat in is still there). On a tour,
you can see the Senate Building's 1901 Grand Staircase (don't forget to look up to
see the state's seal depicted in stained glass in the skylight). Restoration of more
than sixty rooms in the capitol was completed in 1996. You can sit a spell in one of
the many rooms while sessions are in progress and watch our government at work.
You may find yourself concluding, as former Ohio governor and current U.S. Senator
George Voinovich did, that "visiting the Statehouse is one of the best ways to edu-
cate young children and other visitors on what it means to be an Ohioan."

Amazing Ohio Facts

The lowest point in Ohio is the Ohio River.

Columbus's historic German Village is the nation's largest privately funded
restoration district.

The highest point in Ohio is Campbell Hill, Bellefontaine (1,550 feet).

Ohio Theatre (ages 5 and up) 🎵
39 East State Street; (614) 469–0939; www.capa.com/columbus.

Across from the capitol on Broad Street is another restored masterpiece, the Ohio Theatre. The Loew's theater chain spent nearly $2 million to rebuild and redecorate what stands today as a premier example—one of the few remaining in the country—of the golden age of vaudeville and silent movies. The first sound movie, *The Tempest*, starring John Barrymore, was shown here in 1929.

The lavishly restored 2,779-seat, Baroque-style theater is adorned with gold-leafed trimmings and Tiffany chandeliers. Columbus residents raised funds to buy the beloved theater just minutes—literally, as the bulldozer was driving down the street—before the wrecking ball was to begin demolition in the late 1960s. Since then, using volunteer labor, donations, and matching funds, the Ohio has been transformed into a lively theater of the performing arts with a full schedule of events, including a popular summer classic movie series that draws families from all over Franklin County and beyond. The theater is also home to the Columbus Symphony Orchestra, BalletMet Columbus, and a Broadway comedy and musical series, making it the busiest performing-arts facility in the state of Ohio.

Barber Museum and the Barbering Hall of Fame
(ages 5 and up)
2 South High Street, Canal Winchester; (614) 833–9931; www.edjeffersbarber museum.com. Hours by appointment. Free.

It's a classic scene right out of Norman Rockwell—the little boy, his first haircut. If you'd like to relive those simpler days, check out the quirky Barber Museum and Hall of Fame. Ed Jeffers, a former barber, now serves as the curator of this unusual collection, housed not far from Columbus in Canal Winchester. Jeffers spent the past forty years collecting more than 500 shaving mugs, some sixty rare barber poles, barber chairs, and lots of other memorabilia such as tools, scissors, and tons of tonic.

Columbus City Center Mall (all ages) 🛍
111 South Third Street; (614) 221–4900; www.shopcitycenter.com.

Looking for a souvenir of your stay? Pick up anything your heart desires at the $200 million Columbus City Center Mall, adjacent to the Hyatt Hotel across from the capitol complex. Kids won't be able to resist spending their allowance at the clever Imaginarium or the Great Train Store, which is overflowing with train memorabilia of all kinds by Lionel or Thomas the Tank Engine.

The downtown shopping center—one of the few in the country—has more than 150 shops for all budgets, including several of Columbus native and Limited founder Leslie H. Wexner's stores. There's also Macy's and Ohio-based Lazarus as well as national restaurants and boutiques. The ever-tempting A Show of Hands gallery features the best of Ohio-made arts and crafts.

German Village (all ages)

588 South Third Street; (614) 221–8888; www.germanvillage.org. Daily tours offered in summer; volunteers available to help design self-guided tours other times of the year.

Just 6 blocks south of the state capitol via Third Street is German Village, a friendly neighborhood that earned a spot on the National Register of Historic Places in 1975 because of the quaint brick homes set along its narrow cobblestoned streets. German immigrants settled the 230-acre area in the mid-1800s; it was narrowly saved from a freeway expansion and the wrecking ball in the 1950s. Curious about old-time Columbus? This is a great place to get an idea of how city residents lived in the nineteenth century.

Today it's home to young urban professionals and others who prize the area's heritage and historic charm. Wanderers in German Village find well-tended cottages and stately mansions with flower-filled window boxes and wrought-iron gates. Chic coffeehouses sit side by side with quilt shops, neighborhood pubs, and authentic German bakeries.

Ideal for walking (but not always for parking), German Village is one of Columbus's major attractions, drawing more than 100,000 visitors a year. More than just a pretty piece of restored Americana, this is a working neighborhood, with businesses from supermarkets and dry cleaners to antiques shops and bookstores. Strudel is still sold at Juergen's Bakery and Restaurant on South Fourth Street (614–224–6858) and bratwurst at Schmidt's Sausage Haus, on Kussuth Street, where they're also famous for their bet-you-can't-eat-it-all cream puffs (614–444–6808). Thurn's, on Third, is an old-fashioned and still-popular lunch counter.

Another landmark is Diebel's, where the spicy sausage and sauerkraut are legendary and where even the kids get into the rollicking, good-time spirit during weekly polka parties and weekend sing-alongs. In the middle of it all is peaceful Schiller Park, twenty-three acres of greensward in the middle of the district's tree-lined streets and home to many of the area's bed-and-breakfast inns. Today this urban oasis has an amphitheater, tennis and basketball courts, a playground, jogging paths, and a recently restored lake. Pick up some sandwiches from nearby Katzinger's Deli (475 South Third), an area landmark voted "Best Deli in America" by *Bon Appetit* magazine, and dine alfresco at one of the park's shaded tables.

Take home a piece of German Village with a visit to the Golden Hobby Shop (630 South Third Street; 614–645–8329). Housed in a former school, it sells crafts made by senior citizens from the area, from wooden shelves and hard-to-find old-fashioned toys such as tops and hand-painted wooden airplanes to intricately pieced quilts and beautiful knits.

Avid readers of all ages can get lost in the nooks and crannies of the Book Loft (631 South Third Street; 614–464–1774; open daily 10:00 A.M. to 10:00 P.M.), where the store takes up an entire city block and where negotiating the twenty-five rooms of discounted paperbacks and hardcovers requires a map—and a limitless credit

Ohio **Learning Adventures**

The Great Ohio Adventures in Learning (GOAL) program from the Ohio Department of Development's Division of Travel and Tourism has everything families need to keep kids entertained—and to keep them learning while they're at it. More than 300 entertaining and educational travel sites include the opportunity to tour a factory, take a virtual tour on the Underground Railroad, or peek into the life of some of America's greatest presidents.

Divided into twelve categories, the GOAL routes include African American Ohio Heritage, Arts in Ohio, Natural Ohio, Presidential Ohio, Literary Ohio, Made in Ohio, Native Ohio, Science and Technology, and Transportation.

Families can find a complete directory online at www.ohiotourism.com under Kids Stuff/GOAL. For convenient travel planning, the directory lists attractions geographically too. Information is also available from (800) BUCKEYE (282–5393).

card. The selection of children's books and tapes is second to none. The quirky Hausfrau Haven, also on Third Street, has unusual greeting cards, soft drinks, fine wines, and a renowned homemade fudge. Mind the kids while you visit, however; playful signs warn that unattended children will be sold.

You might even see lederhosen on some natives during special events. The neighborhood is the spotlight of the annual Haus und Garten Tour the last Sunday in June as well as the Candlelight Garten Tour in August and a Merry Christmas Tour of Homes. It's also home to the city's wildly popular Oktoberfest, held (paradoxically) in early September. Adults can stamp along to oompah-pah music and sample local brews; the younger set can participate in an ice-cream eating contest or the cream-puff stuff, thrill to the **free** kiddie rides in the Kinderplatz, or enjoy family-style entertainment, including performances by Opera Columbus, the Columbus Junior Theater, and Grandparents Living Theater. It's wunderbar!

Center of Science & Industry (COSI) (all ages)

333 West Broad Street; (614) 228–2674, (888) 819–COSI; www.cosi.org. Open 10:00 A.M. to 5:00 P.M. Wednesday through Saturday and noon to 5:00 P.M. Sunday. Adults $$$, kids ages two to twelve $$.

Had enough history? It's back to the future at the popular Ohio Center of Science and Industry, known affectionately as COSI, a short walk away on Broad Street. It's hard to tell who's having more fun here—the children or the so-called adults. Dedicated to the conviction that science can be fun (you'll be convinced, too, after a visit), Ohio's top science center and one of only twenty-two such centers worldwide attracts more than 700,000 "kids" of all ages from all over the world each year.

Known by its nickname, "The Fascination Station," COSI Columbus is a 300,000-square-foot science center that opened originally in 1964 in the former Columbus Veteran's Hall. In the more than forty years since its founding, the center has served eighteen million visitors on-site and more through its innovative COSI on Wheels program used in Ohio and seven other surrounding states.

The museum moved to its current location in 1999. Like the original building, the new building included a historic reuse. Once the home of the city's Old Central High School, the new design and architecture are the work of world-renowned architect Arata Isozaki and are like no other place in the world. Located in the heart of downtown, it includes eight interactive learning worlds filled with challenging and intriguing exhibits for all ages. From Rat Basketball (move over Michael Jordan!) to SPACE (the Final Frontier), COSI specializes in science spelled F-U-N.

Exhibits are spread out over three levels and include Big Science Park, Gadgets, Life, Little Kidspace, Ocean, Space and Progress, and two areas featuring traveling exhibits. Special exhibitions include Risk: Live and Learn, Reptiles Go Wild, and Star Wars, opening in June 2006. There's also the Midwest's only motion simulator, adventures in agriculture, and the world's first high-wire unicycle. There's also an outdoor science park, three theaters, a restaurant, and a gift shop.

Franklin Park Conservatory & Botanical Garden (all ages) 🏛️ 🌿

1777 East Broad Street; (614) 645–8733, (800) 214–7275; www.fpconservatory.org. Open 10:00 A.M. to 5:00 P.M. Tuesday through Sunday and Wednesday until 8:00 P.M. Adults $$, kids ages four to eleven $. Free admission to Palm House and bonsai collection.

After the excitement of COSI, you may want to wind down with a visit to the peaceful Franklin Park Conservatory & Botanical Garden, also on Broad Street. Located on twenty-eight acres within the lush eighty-eight-acre Franklin Park, the conservatory opened to the public in 1895 and was modeled after London's Crystal Palace. It

Wonderful **Wendy's**

After a fun-filled day at COSI, it's time to refuel. The first Wendy's restaurant, opened by the late R. David Thomas on November 15, 1969, is located across the street from COSI. Today there are more than 4,000 Wendy's Old Fashioned Hamburger restaurants worldwide, but few compare to the original, complete with the signature blue-and-white-striped decor and pictures of the chain's red-haired, pig-tailed namesake. Indulge in a cool chocolatey Frosty, or grab a burger and some fries before heading to your next stop.

underwent a dramatic change in 1992, when a $14 million expansion was built for AmeriFlora '92, a floral celebration marking Christopher Columbus's discovery of America.

This pleasing mix of glass and grace is home to approximately 10,000 plants representing more than 1,200 species. They're displayed in six climatic areas: the Himalayan Mountain Room, the Tropical Rain Forest, the Desert, the Pacific Island Water Garden, the Tree Fern Forest, and the Cloud Forest. Show your kids where coffee comes from; watch gardeners clip the delicate, tiny trees in the bonsai garden; or relax under the tall palms in the Palm House, also a popular spot for weddings. Young horticulturists get a kick out of the Shaving Brush Tree, named because its flowers resemble old-fashioned shaving brushes.

Also be sure to check out the Chihuly glass exhibition, which is part of the permanent collection. The conservatory is the only public botanical garden to own a signature collection of Chihuly's work.

Topiary Garden (all ages) 🏕️ 🌿

480 East Town Street; (614) 645–0197; www.topiarygarden.org. Open daily dawn to dusk. Free.

Think Disney World does great things with shrubs? Forget simple mouse ears and elephants. Green thumbs of all ages also congregate at the downtown Topiary Garden on East Town Street, part of the Deaf School Park. This fanciful landscape created by sculptor James T. Mason depicts pointillist painter Georges Seurat's *Sunday Afternoon on the Island of La Grande Jatte* and includes fifty-two larger-than-life human figures, eight boats, three dogs, and a monkey. It's the only topiary garden in the country to include human figures—some up to 12 feet tall—and the only one in the world that is an interpretation of a painting. Watch gardeners snip and clip the figures into shape, and who knows what you'll be inspired to do with the bushes back home.

Columbus Museum of Art (ages 2 and up) 🖼️

480 East Broad Street; (614) 221–6801; www.columbusmuseum.org. Open daily 10:00 A.M. to 5:30 P.M., Thursday until 8:30 P.M. Adults $$, kids ages five to eleven $, free for those under five. Free on Thursday.

Miniature Monets won't want to miss the Columbus Museum of Art, closer to downtown on Broad Street. Ohio's first museum is known for its innovative traveling exhibitions and its small but excellent permanent collection (including the breathtaking $80 million Sirak Collection). The museum offers a relaxing respite from the city streets and a well-loved impressionist collection. Bright abstractions such as Frank Stella's *Nasielsk III* or *La Vecchia Dell'Orto* (The Witch of the Garden) and Deborah Butterfield's life-size horse of welded steel are family favorites and provide inspiration to young artists. Look, too, for works by two eminent Columbus artists, realist George Bellows and folk artist Elijah Pierce, and for Eye Spy—Adventures in Art, an interactive exhibit for kids and families. The museum is worth a stop just for the well-stocked Museum Shop, which has a great children's corner with everything from Madeline books to make-your-own-masterpiece kits.

Thurber House (ages 10 and up) 🏛

77 Jefferson Avenue; (614) 464–1032; www.thurberhouse.org. Open daily noon to 4:00 P.M. for free; guided tours $.

Not far from the museum is the Thurber House, onetime home of James Thurber, one of America's best-loved humorists. Older kids and would-be writers and cartoonists are enchanted with this modest home, where Thurber lived during his college days (from 1913 to 1917) with his parents, two brothers, numerous pet dogs, and an occasional relative. Many of Thurber's best-known stories (available for sale in the small shop, once the dining room) are set here; it's here where the alarms sound at night, where the electricity leaks, and where the bed has been known to fall unexpectedly.

This is no velvet-rope house museum, although artifacts and memorabilia from Thurber's long career fill the rooms. Today it's a lively writers' center and the popular site of summer Literary Picnics and winter Evenings with Authors series.

Wexner Center for the Arts (ages 5 and up) 🎨

1871 North High Street on the Ohio State University campus; (614) 292–3535; www.wexarts.org. Open Tuesday, Wednesday, and Sunday 11:00 A.M. to 6:00 P.M.; Thursday through Saturday until 8:00 P.M. Free.

Columbus is a town that prides itself on its strong support of the arts. One of the best places in the city to see cutting-edge visual arts is the Wexner Center. Located near the heart of the Ohio State University (OSU) campus and dedicated to vanguard artistic activity, it opened in 1989 and was designed to be "an architectural event" and a center for the presentation and study of contemporary arts. With a multidisciplinary approach including exhibitions, media arts, performing arts, and education, the center encourages continuous exploration and research in the arts. An extensive $15.8 million renovation was completed in fall of 2005.

The four galleries host traveling exhibitions from modern art museums around the world, including the Museum of Modern Art in New York, the Walker Art Center in Minneapolis, and the Centre Georges Pompidou in Paris, as well as a popular avant-garde film series.

Ohio Authors

James Thurber is just one of many well-known Ohio authors. Others include William Dean Howells, Ambrose Bierce, Paul Laurence Dunbar, Harriet Beecher Stowe, Sherwood Anderson, Zane Grey, and popular columnist Erma Bombeck.

Columbus Clippers (ages 4 and up)

1155 West Mound Street; (614) 462–5250 or www.clippersbaseball.com for tickets and schedules.

Ohio State football is big business in Columbus and across the state. Buckeyes from all over the country make pilgrimages to the campus, which is the site of tailgate parties and intense rivalry on crisp autumn weekends. But there's also a lot of other sports action in town. Although invitations from the major leagues haven't piled up at Columbus's door, city residents take pride in their AAA baseball club, the Columbus Clippers, a farm team for the New York Yankees. They play at the 15,000-seat Clipper Stadium, not far from downtown, from May through October.

The Clipper Stadium is the site of popular birthday parties where, for a small per-person fee, guests receive a reserved seat, hot dog, and refreshments, and the birthday boy or girl gets his or her name on the scoreboard, a **free** personalized baseball card, and a visit from the team's mascot, Captain Clipper. Regular special events include Kids' Club Night every Monday, with **free** general admission for children twelve and younger, and Fireworks Night, with a spectacular fireworks extravaganza following Friday games. Family Day at the Ball Park is one of the best deals around, when the whole family (two adults and up to four children eighteen and younger) is admitted for just $5.00.

Ohio State Fair (all ages)

East Eleventh Avenue. For schedules and more information, call (800) BUCKEYE (282–5393); www.ohiostatefair.com. $$, those under age five are free. A ride-all-day wristband is $$$.

Being the state capital, Columbus is the appropriate home of the Ohio State Fair. If your kids think milk comes from a plastic jug, it's time to check out this annual event, which celebrated its 150th anniversary in 2003. Grab your "fair" share of fun as the state goes "whole hog" with an overflowing cornucopia of fun-filled activities and Ohio-grown riches at the Ohio State Fairgrounds, not far from downtown Columbus.

The chance to bring home the blue ribbon brings out the best the state has to offer in livestock, agriculture, horticulture, and the creative arts. And there's always the exciting chance to see things such as the largest pumpkin or to taste award-winning homemade apple pie and stick-to-the-roof-of-your-mouth cotton candy, a fair staple.

City kids will love watching the grooming in the livestock area, where more than 20,000 spanking-clean farm animals are exhibited, or the hilarious racing pigs contest. Horse lovers head for the All-Breed Horse Show, the nation's largest, featuring more than twenty-seven breeds. Other exciting attractions include a championship rodeo; truck and tractor pulls; Hollywood stunt shows; motocross races; a classic midway filled with awe-inspiring rides, games, and food concessions; and a petting zoo and the **free** Kiddie Park. Grab a corn dog and buy a wristband that entitles you to ride all day long, and the day is yours.

Other family fun highlights include the dazzling Laser Light Adventure, performed **free** outside the coliseum nightly; the Olde Tyme Big Top Circus; and Barn Tours. At night, wind down with **free** entertainment at Celeste Center, featuring some of the greatest names in the business. Hundreds of **free** performances will have you singing along and tapping your feet. And if you're feeling really adventurous, check out the Ejection Seat, which shoots volunteers fourteen stories into the air in just three seconds.

For a great deal, head for the fair on one of the annual Family Value Days, when kids younger than age twelve are admitted **free** and parents get in for the children's fee.

The Optometry Museum (ages 3 and up)

338 West Tenth Avenue; (614) 292–2788. Open Monday through Friday from 8:00 A.M. to 5:00 P.M. Free.

At Ohio State University a small but fascinating museum occupies Fry Hall, where some famous people make spectacles of themselves. Founded by a professor at Ohio State University who sent out hundreds of letters to local and national figures asking for their old glasses, this museum includes specs and sunglasses that once belonged to notables from Elvis to writer Stephen King. Nearly seventy-five pairs (often accompanied by a photo of the celebrity wearing them) fill this optometry museum. Also included are odd-looking gadgets, a refractor from the end of the nineteenth century, a retinoscope, and early examples of wooden frames from Europe and China.

Ohio Historical Center (all ages)

1982 Velma Avenue; (614) 297–2300, (800) 653–6446; www.ohiohistory.org. Hours vary with season. Adults $$, kids ages six to twelve $.

Across from the fairgrounds off Interstate 71 you'll also find the Ohio Historical Center, now in its thirty-fifth year. Who needs a time machine when you can travel from the Ice Age to the Space Age in just a few hours? Step back in time with a visit to the center's extensive collection and its adjacent re-created Civil War–era village.

The center, housed in a distinctive, modern-looking building visible from I–71, packs a million years of history into 600,000 square feet of space. Permanent exhibits and varied displays examine the area's prehistory, history, and natural history. Meet the state's oldest inhabitants in "The First Ohioans" display, with materials from the state's prehistoric cultures. Because of this exhibit, the *Smithsonian Guide to Historic America* named the center "the finest museum in America devoted to pre-European history."

Other fascinating displays include Ohio: Two Centuries of Change, which explores the state from 1770 to 1970, encompassing early settlement to the civil rights era. Here you'll find everything from a re-creation of a mid-nineteenth-century carriage company (complete with huge pulleys) and a 1907 fire engine to a working millstone and a jazzy 1957 jukebox that once graced an Ohio diner.

The Nature of Ohio, one of the center's newest exhibits, has drawn rave reviews from families. The exhibit's entrance is guarded by a huge Conway Mastodon. A favorite with generations of children, the 10,000-year-old elephant-like skeleton was found in 1894 beneath 4 feet of swampy ground in Clark County, Ohio, and has tusks that measure 9½ feet long. Kids also like to congregate by the two-headed calf from 1910, the 1926 Egyptian mummy, and the rock and mineral displays.

Another popular exhibit traces animals native to the state that are now extinct—including bison, once abundant in Ohio, which vanished during early settlement. Stop by the well-stocked gift shop on the way out and peruse the many Ohio-related items, including Civil War caps, city puzzles, and Indian mound replicas. Don't leave without letting the kids taste one of the nine flavors of rock candy for sale. This old-fashioned treat still satisfies a modern sweet tooth.

Anthony-Thomas Candy Company (ages 4 and up)

1777 Arlingate Lane; (614) 274–8405; www.anthony-thomas.com. Tours by appointment on Tuesday and Thursday 9:30 A.M. to 2:30 P.M. Free.

Willie Wonka fans might want to head west on Interstate 270, where, not far from downtown, they'll find the Anthony-Thomas Candy Company. This longtime city institution and one of the largest family-owned candy-making facilities in the United States has been making chocolate in Columbus since 1952, when it was founded in a local kitchen a long way away from the current 152,000-square-foot factory.

You'll be licking your lips while you tour the facility. In about an hour, tour guides explain the candy-making process from start to finish. You'll watch workers create candy fillings in huge copper kettles as you walk along the comfortable, glass-enclosed overhead passageway. Guides point out several production lines (the company has the ability to produce 25,000 pounds of chocolate in just one shift), as well as the unusual silver pipes that carry liquid chocolate through the factory. The tour ends in the 2,500-square-foot retail store (there are fifteen other retail stores in the Columbus area).

Short **North**

Columbus's version of New York's Soho can be found in the Short North Commercial District, which bridges downtown and Ohio State University along U.S. Highway 23, also known as High Street. Galleries here sell everything from fine to folk art as well as vintage clothing and funky souvenirs. You'll also find coffeehouses and a wide range of restaurants. A gallery hop the first Saturday of the month showcases the many offerings, with open doors and free refreshments and activities.

Seat of Your Pants **Tour**

For a different perspective on the city, saddle up for a ride on the Olentangy-Scioto Bikeway, which runs from downtown through the suburbs. Along the way, it passes popular sites such as German Village, the *Santa Maria*, and Antrim Lake, which has a popular loop used by walkers, joggers, and in-line skaters. For more information contact the City of Columbus Recreation and Parks Department at (614) 645–3300.

Where to Eat

Buckeye Hall of Fame Cafe, 14210 Olentangy River Road; (614) 291–2233. Not surprisingly, this sports-minded cafe is decorated with Ohio State University memorabilia. $

Cap City Diner, 1299 Olentangy River Road; (614) 291–3663. This fun eatery highlights both traditional and creative diner fare. Great service. $–$$

Engine House No. 5, 121 Thurman Avenue, German Village; (614) 443–4877. If you're looking for a place to celebrate an older child's birthday, consider Engine House No. 5, known for its seafood. It's housed in a restored firehouse and features servers sliding down a gleaming brass fire pole, complete with celebratory cakes and sparklers. It's fun the rest of the year, too. $$

94th Aero Squadron, 5030 Sawyer Road; (614) 237–8887. Aviation buffs of all ages love this French farmhouse restaurant with its aviation theme and dining room overlooking the airport's runways. Don't miss the delectable desserts, including the upside-down apple walnut pie. $$

Where to Stay

Courtyard by Marriott, 35 West Spring Street, downtown Columbus; (614) 228–3200. A more cosmopolitan version of this national chain, with 149 rooms and upscale decor. Features include a whirlpool, small indoor pool, on-site dining room with great breakfast buffet, coin laundry, and free and pay movies. Four rooms have kitchens with microwaves and refrigerators. $$

Holiday Inn City Center, 175 East Town Street; (614) 221–3281. This newly renovated full-service hotel in downtown is best known with families for its "Kids Eat Free" deal, which offers a free kid's meal when an adult entree is purchased. Highlights include 278 rooms, a small indoor pool, an on-site restaurant, free movies, and in-room coffeemakers. $–$$

Holiday Inn Worthington, 175 Hutchinson Avenue; (614) 885–3334. Handy location near downtown with 306 rooms. Convenient for trips to the nearby Center of Science & Industry (COSI), Columbus Zoo, and the IMAX theater located across the street. Free movies and in-room coffee are featured. $–$$

For More Information

Greater Columbus Convention and Visitors Bureau, 90 North High Street, Columbus 43215-3014; (800) 345–2657; www.experiencecolumbus.com.

Powell

Columbus Zoo and Aquarium (all ages) 🐾

9990 Riverside Drive; (614) 645–3550; www.colszoo.org. Open daily year-round from 9:00 A.M. to 5:00 P.M. Memorial Day through Labor Day hours are 9:00 A.M. to 6:00 P.M. Adults $$, children ages two to eleven $, free for children under two.

When the Columbus Zoo, located northwest of the city in Powell, was established in 1927, it cost a dime to enter. Today admission is slightly more, but you still get a lot of fun for your buck.

Like many of its large and powerful animals, the zoo was tiny at birth, housing a small collection of donated animals. From this humble beginning it has developed into one of the fastest-growing and most highly acclaimed zoos in the nation.

The zoo has had plenty of firsts: In 1956 it made headlines with the birth of Colo, the first gorilla born in captivity. Since then, generations of other lowland gorillas have been born here. The zoo also won international recognition for its breeding programs and its protection of many rare and endangered species. In addition, it's known for its former director, Jack Hanna, who was seen for years cavorting with Johnny Carson and a parade of animal guests on *The Tonight Show*, and who is a regular visitor on *Good Morning America*.

Today the zoo is home to more than 700 species and 11,000 specimens spread out on rolling, well-manicured grounds. Although you'll find plenty of the "regulars," such as lions, tigers, and bears, it's also one of only four U.S. zoos to exhibit bonobos, also known as pygmy chimpanzees. And it's one of the few zoos in the nation to permanently exhibit koalas, which are featured in an Australian exhibit that also has wallabies, emus, and black swans.

Pint-size animal lovers won't want to miss riding on the bumpy back of an Asian camel (the less adventurous can take pony rides in the Kids Zoo), paddling about the Scioto River on the zoo's stern-wheeler, or exploring the indoor Discovery Reef, with more than 400 colorful species—including stingrays and sharks—in vast tanks, and a special tidepool where curious kids can touch starfish, sea urchins, and other aquatic creatures. Head for the playscape when your miniature safarians need to blow off a little steam; it has ropes for climbing, a wooden ship to man, and more.

The latest exhibition opened in May of 2003 and features an adventure to the Islands of Southeast Asia. You'll see Komodo dragons, white-handed gibbons, orangutans, black swans, and more on a leisurely boat ride or from a number of walking trails. Popular seasonal events include Boo at the Zoo in October and the Wildlight Wonderland, when more than 750,000 twinkling lights, displays, and rides for children welcome the holidays.

On Safari **in Columbus**

Dinosaurs, elephants, airplanes, space ships—you name it. Nate, my teenager, was once fascinated by anything that dwarfed him in size and moved. So he was especially thrilled a few years ago during a visit to the 400-acre Columbus Zoo when he was offered the chance to ride an elephant. He looked a little nervous as he was helped up onto the huge beast's back but soon recovered his nerve as a zookeeper led him around the small ring, and he smiled and waved at the onlookers crowding the area. He still talks about it. It was well worth the extra couple of dollars.

Wyandot Lake Adventure Park (all ages)

Sawmill Road, off Interstate 270; (614) 889–9283; www.sixflags.com. Hours vary with the season. Adults $$$$, kids 42 inches and shorter $$$.

Does watching sea lions and penguins cavort make your budding zoologists wish for some wet-and-wild adventures of their own? Luckily, the zoo is adjacent to the eighteen-acre Wyandot Lake Adventure Park, which offers "good clean fun" from May through September. Grab the suits, the sunscreen, and the camera (just make sure it's waterproof) and catch a wave.

Nothing quenches a thirst for fun like a day at Wyandot Lake, where you can take the sizzle out of summer. Get drenched by a burst of tropical showers and unpredictable geysers as you weave through the winding turns and white-water rapids of Zuma Falls. Blast through the slippery dark as you speed down six stories of tunnels in less than thirty seconds on the twisting and turning JetStream ride. When you need a relaxing break, kick back, grab an inner tube, and enjoy a lazy float down 850-foot-long Canoochee Creek or challenge the ocean surf of the Wild Tide's million-gallon wave pool. With more than sixty great rides and attractions, Wyandot Lake is among Ohio's best water parks.

Little ones get into the watery action with a swim in the Tadpool or while exploring Buccaneer Bay, a multicolor, multiactivity water playground with geysers and gizmos built just for kids. There are even offerings for landlubbers, including eighteen classic dry rides that include a wooden roller coaster; an authentic, antique 1914 carousel; a Kiddieland full of miniature boat and car rides; minigolf; go-karts; and live entertainment.

Having too good a time to go home? Dive-in Movie Nights let guests enjoy comedy and adventure films while floating and splashing in the wave pool or lounging on the shores of Parrot Cove. You'll never prefer the home VCR or DVD again.

Delaware

Olentangy Indian Caverns (ages 4 and up) 🏛 🎦

1779 Home Road; (740) 548–7917; www.olentangyindiancaverns.com. Open daily April through October from 9:30 A.M. to 5:00 P.M. Adults $$, kids ages seven to fifteen $, those under seven are free.

Not far north of Columbus via U.S. Highway 23 and Interstate 270 are the Olentangy Indian Caverns. For a better understanding of the people who settled this part of the country, a visit here is a must.

Formed millions of years ago by an underground river cutting through solid limestone, the caverns are now a maze of winding passages and spacious underground rooms. There is evidence that the Wyandot Indians used the caverns as a haven from the weather and their enemies. One of the larger rooms contains the Council Rock, believed to be used for tribal ceremonies. The caverns were discovered by J. M. Adams, whose oxen broke loose from his wagon train in 1821 and were later found dead at the bottom of the cavern's entrance. Adams's name and the date of his discovery, inscribed on the wall, can be seen to this day.

Miniature explorers love to descend the concrete stairs 55 feet into the cool, three-level caverns or tour the cave museum, which houses Native American artifacts and geological displays. Let the kids spend their allowance in the Native American–themed gift shop; afterward, enjoy a picnic lunch, explore adjacent Frontier Land (have your name printed on a WANTED poster in the print shop), or relax with a round of minigolf while the kids hit the playground.

For More Information

Delaware County Convention and Visitors Bureau, (888) 345–6446; www.visitdelohio.com.

Ohio's **Presidential Path**

Ohio can boast eight U.S. presidents, more than any other state in the union: William Henry Harrison, Ulysses S. Grant, Rutherford B. Hayes, James Garfield, Benjamin Harrison, William McKinley, William Howard Taft, and Warren Harding.

Marion

Warren Harding Home & Memorial (ages 6 and up) 🔵

380 Mount Vernon Avenue; (740) 387–9630, (800) 600–6894; www.ohiohistory.org.
Open weekends only; Saturday 9:30 A.M. to 5:00 P.M. and Sunday noon to 5:00 P.M.
Adults $$, children ages six to twelve $, five and under **free.**

What little boy—and more and more, what little girl—hasn't grown up wanting to be
president? Ohio has given the country many presidents, including Warren G. Harding,
a Marion native and the country's twenty-ninth president. During the 1920 presiden-
tial campaign, he addressed voters from the wide front porch of his 1891 Victorian-
style boyhood home. It later became known as his "front-porch" campaign.

Indulge your would-be statesmen and stateswomen with a visit to this impressive
presidential home and museum. Today your family can take a guided tour of the
Harding home, which has been meticulously restored and holds authentic furniture,
statues, and clothing used by Warren Harding and his wife, Florence, from 1891 to
1920. The library was renovated in 2005. The nearby Harding Memorial, located
south of Marion on Highway 423 and set in a peaceful ten-acre landscaped park, was
built from public donations, including dime contributions from state schoolchildren.

Marion County Museum of History/Wyandot Popcorn Museum
(ages 3 and up) 🔵

169 East Church Street; (740) 387–4255; www.marionohio.com. Open Wednesday
through Sunday from 1:00 to 4:00 P.M. May through October; open weekends only
November through April. **Free.**

Marion isn't all about presidents and politics: It's also about popcorn. The zany Wyan-
dot Popcorn Museum features a three-ring circus tent full of old-fashioned fun with a
priceless collection of antique popcorn poppers, peanut roasters, concession trucks,
and vintage popcorn wagons dating between 1890 and 1940. George Brown, a
museum board member and former chairman of the board of the Marion-based
Wyandot Company, maker of popcorn snacks, was instrumental in
putting the collection together. Today it's the only one of its type
in the world.

Rare models include the 1915 Holcomb & Hoke, the earliest
automated popper; and the 1927 Cretors Eclipse, the first all-
electric popper. There are forty-eight other vintage and restored
popcorn machines in the former U.S. Post Office. You also can
see demonstrations of ten steam engines, two of which are
spring driven. Of course, **free** popcorn is served daily.

Lawrence Orchards (all ages)

2634 Smeltzer Road; (740) 389–3019; www.lawrenceorchards.com. Hours vary with season.

Fall is the perfect time to visit a U-pick farm. Lawrence Orchards in Marion has been serving families since 1921. This family-run orchard and farm market has a lock on home-grown freshness and is the location for the popular Orchard Harvest Craft Fair in August and the rollicking Applefest in September.

Where to Stay

Fairfield Inn by Marriott, 227 Jamesway; (740) 389–6636. This fifty-seven-room hotel has spacious guest rooms and free and pay movies. Some rooms have easy chairs. $

Marion Comfort Inn, 256 Jamesway; (740) 389–5552. This inn has fifty-six rooms and a whirlpool, pool, and game room. Rooms have free and pay movies; some have microwaves and refrigerators. $–$$

For More Information

Marion Area Convention and Visitors Bureau, (800) 371–6688, (740) 389–9770; www.visitmarionohio.com.

Circleville

Circleville Pumpkin Festival (all ages)

159 East Franklin Street; (740) 474–7000; www.pumpkinshow.com. Free.

Every school kid studying American history knows that the Pilgrims ate pumpkin pie at their second, not their first, Thanksgiving dinner. Yet even before that, settlers were making pumpkin stew and pumpkin soup, even drinking pumpkin beer. The world's largest festival honoring this Halloween trademark began in 1903 as a small exhibit of pumpkins and corn fodder. Today it has grown into a four-day extravaganza of parades and contests known as the Circleville Pumpkin Festival, held in Circleville, 25 miles south of Columbus.

For several days each October the pumpkin festival bills itself as "The Greatest Free Show on Earth." The festival lures hundreds of thousands of "pumpkin people" with displays of giant pumpkins (some as large as 400 pounds!) and the world's largest pumpkin pie (one year it weighed 350 pounds and was 5 feet in diameter). Kids get into the fun with contests for the best pumpkin poster and decorations, best carved and painted pumpkin heads, best funny facial expressions, and strangest hat.

Ever tasted pumpkin fudge or pumpkin burgers? How 'bout french-fried pumpkin chips? You can here. There are also booths selling pumpkin delicacies; agricultural exhibits; clowns; bands; rides; games; and even a great "pumpkin tree" in the center of town.

Utica

Ye Olde Mill (ages 2 and up) 🐘🚙🏛

P.O. Box 588, Utica 43080; (740) 892–3921; www.velveticecream.com. Open daily from 11:00 A.M. to 9:00 P.M. May through October.

Ye Olde Mill in Utica, near Newark, is home to a nineteenth-century gristmill that features the state's only ice-cream museum, an ice-cream viewing gallery, a water-wheel, and an 1817 mill-turned-ice-cream parlor.

Tours are offered from the visitor center on the hour between 11:00 A.M. and 3:00 P.M. During the tour you'll learn about the mill's history as a stop on the Underground Railroad.

The adjacent picnic park includes a twenty-acre scenic pond, perfect for alfresco licks and meals, and a popular playground area. The mill is the site of the popular Buckeye Tree Festival, held each September, which includes Ohio artisans and craftspeople dressed in the clothing of the era who demonstrate aspects of life on the Ohio frontier. Other special events include the ever-popular Ice Cream Festival in May and Fall Harvest Days. Pony rides, horse-drawn wagons, and zoo animals are especially popular with the kids, as are the displays of the Order of the Arrow, a Boy Scout group that emphasizes Native American folklore, beliefs, costumes, and performances.

Newark

Newark Earthworks (ages 4 and up) 🏛🎒

99 Cooper Avenue; (740) 344–1920, (800) 600–7174; www.ohiohistory.org. Museum admission $, children under six free. Park admission is free.

Do your kids like solving mysteries? Give them a crack at the sixty-six-acre Newark Earthworks, part of what once was the most extensive earthworks in the country. These geometric enclosures were believed to have been used by the Hopewell Indians (1000 B.C. to A.D. 300) for social, religious, and burial ceremonies, but their real purpose remains shrouded in mystery. The Hopewell people lived primarily in central and southern Ohio along the major river valleys such as the Miami, the Scioto, and the Muskingum. Yet despite a strong family structure and a complex way of life, the culture disappeared around A.D. 500–600.

The earthworks are fascinating to explore. The Hopewells' engineering feat is preserved in Wright, Octagon, and Moundbuilders earthworks and Moundbuilders

Ohio Indian Art Museum, the nation's first museum devoted to prehistoric Native American art.

Archaeologists have found pipes and some ceremonial objects at the sites. Necklaces and bracelets were common ornaments, with beads made from pearls or cut from freshwater or marine shells. A number of small figurines excavated from several Hopewell sites show that the women wore knee-length skirts and moccasins, and men wore breechcloths, belts, and moccasins. Both wore garments made of skins and used feathers for headdresses.

The Newark Earthworks cover an area of more than 2 miles. Although the expansion of the city has obliterated parts of the walls and many of the mounds, important sections are preserved in Octagon State Memorial, with 138 acres, and in Moundbuilders State Memorial, with 66.

Within the fifty-acre Octagon Earthworks are small mounds. The Great Circle Earthworks, with conjoined mounds at its center, is located in the Moundbuilders State Memorial. This embankment is approximately 1,200 feet in diameter, with earthen walls ranging from 8 to 14 feet high. Approximately 0.25 mile northeast are the Wright Earthworks, a small section of a large enclosure that was once part of the original Newark works.

For a better understanding of the Hopewell culture and the fascinating people who built these earthworks, stop at the Ohio Indian Art Museum, opened in 1971 at Moundbuilders State Memorial. Objects inside represent the artistic achievements of all known prehistoric cultures in Ohio from 10,000 B.C. to A.D. 1600.

Park It in Ohio

They've always been great, but now the secret is out.

In 1997 Ohio's extensive state park system was the first to win the National Recreation and Park Association's Gold Medal Award for parks and recreation excellence.

Ohio's Department of Natural Resources manages the state's seventy-two parks and beat out parks in Florida, Missouri, and North Carolina for top honors. This is the first time the medal has been awarded to a state park system.

To top it all off, Ohio remains one of the few states in the nation that doesn't charge admission fees to park facilities such as trails, picnic areas, and beaches. The park system celebrated its fiftieth anniversary in 1999.

What does that mean to your average family? Lots of fun on more than 200,000 acres. Included are 8 resort and conference centers, 6 golf courses, 73 beaches, 554 rental cabins, 32 nature centers, and more than 1,000 miles of nature trails—all lots of good reasons to "park it" in Ohio!

Where to Stay

Cherry Valley Lodge, 2299 Cherry Valley Road; (740) 788–1200; www.cherry valleylodge.com. Full-service lodge with beautifully landscaped grounds and 200 comfortable and spacious rooms. Two heated pools, games, and more. $$

The Place off the Square, 50 North Second Street; (740) 322–6455. Cozy hotel downtown boasts guest rooms decorated with candy, flowers, and locally made Longaberger baskets. $

Going **Undercover**

Granville's funky **Lifestyle Museum** (121 South Main Street; 740–587–0373) is more like a crowded attic than a museum. The owners never intended to open a museum; they just saved everything, including a collection of vintage underwear that can be modeled by appointment.

Brownsville

Flint Ridge State Memorial and Museum (ages 4 and up) 🏛 👫
7091 Brownsville Road SE, Glenford; (740) 787–2476; www.ohiohistory.org. Hours vary with season. Park admission free except during special events. Museum admission $, children under six free.

After touring Newark Earthworks, visit Flint Ridge State Memorial, which isn't far away. Many centuries ago, Native American trails from villages and campsites throughout the Midwest converged on this irregular, 10-mile-long range of hills, located between the modern cities of Newark and Zanesville. Prehistoric Native Americans made their way to these hills for a material key to their survival—flint. Today this mineral is also the official gem of the state of Ohio.

Nowhere in the Midwest has better flint been found than in this area. Eventually quarry operations were established to extract the highly prized hard quartz stone. Large hammerstones weighing up to twenty-five pounds were used to wedge natural cracks into the rock.

In 1933 the Ohio Historical Society established the 525-acre memorial to preserve this unusual site, and in 1968 a modern museum was founded over one of the original pits. Here would-be geologists and historians learn about the industrial and human history of this area and visit displays that show the types and location of flint deposits in Ohio, how flint was formed, and modern objects made of this natural resource. Afterward, wander along the asphalt trails that cut through the memorial's nature preserve and wildlife trails. The preserve was created by flint pits that filled up with water and formed temporary ponds and homes for wildlife and plants.

Sugar Grove

Wahkeena Nature Preserve (ages 5 and up) 🕸️ 🏕️ 🌿
**2200 Pump Station Road (County Road 86); (740) 746–8695; www.ohiohistory.org.
Open Wednesday through Sunday from 8:00 A.M. to 4:30 P.M. April through October.
Open by appointment Monday through Friday from November to March. $ per car.**

In 1931 Dr. Frank Warner of Columbus gave his bride, Carmen, a peculiar wedding gift: ninety-four acres of old farmland in southern Fairfield County. Mrs. Warner named her estate *Wahkeena*, a Native American word that means "most beautiful," after a waterfall she had seen in Oregon.

In 1957 Mrs. Warner bequeathed Wahkeena to the Ohio Historical Society "to be used for nature study and as a preserve for birds and other wildlife." Today the 150-acre Wahkeena serves as an outdoor classroom for thousands of the state's young novice naturalists and budding bird-watchers. A log lodge, large pond, and rock formations sculpted from ancient sandstone add to the preserve's calm beauty.

The site regularly hosts hikes, classes, and seminars. Visitors may browse in the nature center or stroll along the serene trails, identifying ferns, trees, and wildflowers with the aid of the site's series of nature guides.

Southwest Ohio

As the flatlands of central Ohio give way to the rolling hills of the southern part of the state, moods—and accents—change. Part Southern hospitality, part pioneer spirit, the southwestern part of the state has a distinctive charm as well as a distinctive topography. Here you can follow in the footsteps of poets and presidents, retrace the travels of Native American tribes or high-flying inventors, and discover a delightful assortment of small towns and sophisticated big cities.

The anchor of southwest Ohio is Cincinnati, also known as "The Queen City," where you can go up a lazy river on an American stern-wheeler, indulge in some sweet/spicy signature chili, or explore charming neighborhoods and first-class attractions.

Khristi's TopPicks for fun in Southwest Ohio

1. Chili-ing out in Cincinnati

2. Going undercover at Ohio Caverns in West Liberty

3. Letting it all hang out at the Great Outdoor Underwear Festival in Piqua

4. Braving the scream machine at Kings Island

5. Exploring Native American history at Sunwatch Village in Dayton

SOUTHWEST OHIO

West Liberty

Piatt Castles (ages 5 and up)

10051 Township Road 47; (513) 465–2821; www.piattcastles.org. Open daily from 11:00 A.M. to 5:00 P.M. May through September and 11:00 A.M. to 4:00 P.M. April and October. Adults $$, kids ages six to twelve $.

A castle is a strange thing to find straddling the border of central and southwest Ohio. But a castle it is—two castles, to be exact, both listed on the National Register of Historic Places. One mile east of West Liberty on Highway 245, not far off Interstate 75, you'll find two of the state's most unusual structures, known collectively as the Piatt Castles.

The Shawnee tribe that once inhabited this land called it Mac-A-Cheek. That name later became the name of the home built by Civil War general and gentleman farmer Abram Sanders Piatt, who built his residence of native limestone and hardwoods. Completed in 1868, the thirty-room Norman French–style chateau is decorated with elaborate woodwork and intricately frescoed ceilings. Castle Mac-A-Chee is filled with Native American artifacts, antique firearms, Civil War relics, and fascinating antiques.

Not to be outdone, his brother Donn Piatt, an editor, writer, and diplomat, built his own castle, known as Mac-O-Chee (your kids won't be able to resist referring to it as the Mac and Cheese castle in honor of that ever-popular entree). Built in two sections, it was started in the late 1860s as a modest Swiss chalet but was then expanded in the late 1870s with the addition of a Flemish-inspired limestone front. It was completed in 1881.

Individual tours of each structure last forty-five minutes and take in all the secret nooks and crannies. The eleven-room Pioneer House, an 1828 log house that was the brothers' boyhood home and a former stop on the Underground Railroad, now is restored and serves as a country gift and antiques shop.

Ohio Caverns (ages 4 and up) 🚻 🍴 🏛

2210 East Highway 245; (513) 465–4017; www.cavern.com/ohiocaverns. Open daily from 9:00 A.M. to 5:00 P.M. April through October and 9:00 A.M. to 4:00 P.M. November through March. Adults $$$, kids five to twelve $$.

Majestic edifices of a more natural kind are the attraction at the Ohio Caverns, not far away on Highway 245. Bring some sweaters—the temperature year-round is a chilly fifty-four degrees. But your kids won't notice—they'll be too busy oohing and aahing over the pure white stalactites and stalagmites (remember: the former grows down, the latter up) and skipping ahead through the cavern's lighted passageways. Ohio Caverns are the largest of all Ohio caves and have been billed as "America's most colorful caverns" because the white crystals create a dramatic effect against the red, black, and gray striations of the cave walls.

After the tour, unwind with a picnic or a nap in the adjacent thirty-five-acre park while the kids cavort in the playground. Guided tours take about an hour and cover almost a mile of underground walking and climbing, which can be hard for younger kids. If you're looking for something a little different, consider the historic tour, which includes parts of the caverns seen by visitors from 1897 to 1925. These sections were reopened in 1997 in honor of the caverns' hundredth anniversary of discovery.

Bellefontaine

Zane Shawnee Caverns (ages 4 and up)

7092 Highway 540; (937) 592–9592. Open daily from 9:00 A.M. to 5:00 P.M. Adults $$, children ages six to twelve $, children under six free.

Ohio is widely known as cave country and as a spelunker's paradise. Many of these underground adventures are found here in the southwestern part of the state. Here you'll find not just one but two great caverns. Zane Shawnee Caverns in Bellefontaine, owned by the Shawnee Nation, is known for its illuminated stalactites and stalagmites as well as its interesting display of "cave pearls." Cave pearls are formed in pools on the cave's floor when small pieces of gravel or grains of sand are dripped on by calcite and "polished" by water. Zane Shawnee features rare white cave pearls.

The caverns reach 132 feet at their deepest point. A forty-minute tour reveals the lore and history of the caves, which were discovered more than a century ago by a hunter whose dog fell into a sinkhole while chasing rabbits. Afterward, set your little explorers loose in the gift shop, relax at the playground at nearby Bluejacket Campground, or enjoy an above-ground picnic.

Logan County Historical Museum (ages 4 and up)

521 East Columbus Avenue; (937) 593–7557. Open May through October from 1:00 to 4:00 P.M. on Wednesday and Friday through Sunday. Admission by donation.

Housed in a spacious 1908 mansion built by a local lumber baron, the museum has a nice collection of vintage toys and a re-created nineteenth-century one-room schoolhouse. Other displays include Native American artifacts, railroad and military memorabilia, and more.

Mad River Mountain Ski Area (ages 4 and up)

Located just off U.S. Highway 33 at Valley Hi; (937) 599–1015, (800) 237–5673; www .skimadriver.com. Rates vary with season.

The Bellefontaine area is also the site of the state's highest point, nearby 1,550-foot Campbell Hill. So it's not surprising to find Mad River Mountain, one of the state's few ski areas, located here.

The mountain has first-class skiing on seventeen trails, with seven lifts and a lift capacity of 8,400 skiers per hour and snow machines capable of producing five tons of snow per minute. Let your kids loose on the bunny hills and snowboard runs or quar-ter pipe while you take to the black-diamond slopes (or vice versa!). Afterward, soak those sore muscles at the Mad River Inn (937–339–1044). Tubing is available, too.

A final piece of area trivia: Bellefontaine (French for "beautiful fountain") had the first concrete streets in America, laid out in 1891. Present-day families still drive on the century-old concrete along downtown Main Street.

Where to Eat

Red Lantern Restaurant, 125 Dowell Avenue; (937) 592–7826. Finger-lickin' fried chicken is the specialty, but there's also a wide variety of other family-oriented entrees and a nice children's menu. On weekends there is a great breakfast buf-fet. $

Where to Stay

Comfort Inn, 260 Northview Drive; (937) 599–5555, (877) 477–5817. The kids will love the large bathrooms, all of which have telephones. Rooms are roomy, too. There's also a coin laundry, free movies, and a few rooms with microwaves, refrigerators, and whirlpools. $

Holiday Inn Bellefontaine, 1135 North Main Street; (937) 593–8515. This inn has 103 spacious rooms, free morning coffee, an on-site dining room, free in-room movies, and a handy coin laundry—a good bet for families on the go. $–$$

Piqua

Great Outdoor Underwear Festival (all ages)
(937) 778–8300. Free.

You know this section of Ohio doesn't take itself too seriously when it has a townwide annual festival devoted to underwear. Just over the border into southwest Ohio is Piqua, which honors its "foundations" each year in mid-October. Started in 1990, the festival offers a "brief" but "revealing" glance at the town's history as the "Underwear Capital of the World."

In the late 1800s, Piqua had ten factories that turned out hosiery, nightwear, and other undergarments. The last one closed in 1993, but the town has never forgotten its distin-guished history. Each year that history takes center stage in the Great Outdoor Underwear Festival that crowds the streets of downtown Piqua for two days on the second weekend of October.

Where else can you cheer on competitors in the "Undy 500," participate in the Drop-Seat Trot (a 5-mile run) or the

Boxer Ball, or even bid at a celebrity underwear auction (Pat Boone, Loni Anderson, and Chubby Checker have participated in the past)? There's also the usual festival fare: food booths, entertainment, and more. *NOTE:* There's been talk of discontinuing this event, so check before heading out.

Piqua Historical Area State Memorial (ages 5 and up) 🏛️ ⛰️
9845 North Hardin Road; (937) 773–2522, (800) 752–2619. Open 9:30 A.M. to 5:00 P.M. Wednesday through Saturday; noon to 5:00 P.M. Sunday. Open weekends only Labor Day through Memorial Day. Adults $$, students age six and up $.

Once the home of John Johnston, an Ohio Canal commissioner and local farmer, the 250-acre farmstead includes an 1815 brick home, cider house, barn, and more restored to their 1829 condition. Top draws for families include the guided tours by costumed interpreters, demonstrations of pioneer crafts, and mule-drawn canal-boat rides. Bring a picnic!

Where to Eat

Terry's Cafeteria, 105 East Greene Street; (937) 778–0566. A homey place with a wide selection of kid-pleasing entrees and luscious homemade desserts. $

Where to Stay

Comfort Inn, 987 East Ash Street; (937) 778–8100. Kids will love the location, which is in the Miami Valley Centre Mall. It has 124 rooms, a whirlpool, and free in-room movies. $–$$

Wilberforce

National Afro-American Museum and Cultural Center
(ages 4 and up) 🖼️
1350 Brush Row Park; (937) 376–4944, (800) 752–2603; www.ohiohistory.org. Open 9:00 A.M. to 5:00 P.M. Tuesday through Saturday. $, free for children under six.

Wilberforce is the home of the National Afro-American Museum and Cultural Center, adjacent to Central State University. Open since 1988, this museum and cultural center is a repository for preservation, study, and interpretation. With an ever-expanding collection of artifacts, manuscripts, and archives spread out over just under 50,000 square feet in a contemporary glass and granite building, the museum reflects the traditions, values, social customs, and experiences of African Americans.

Your children—inheritors of an increasingly diverse world—are sure to gain valuable insights in From Victory to Freedom: Afro-American Life in the Fifties. This exhibit features the award-winning and toe-tapping presentation, Music as Metaphor, which traces Black music of the period and its influence on American culture. Another permanent exhibit chronicles the crucial period in American history from World War II to the present. Recent additions include a landmark exhibition on slavery, a display on African-American dance in history, and art and dolls from the museum's collection.

The museum is also known for its special events, which attract families from all over the state. February features programs in honor of Afro-American History Month; other popular activities include the Oldie but Goodie classic car show in the spring, the Holiday Festival of Black Dolls in October, and a Kwanzaa celebration in December.

Where to Eat and Stay

See Dayton.

Dayton

Dayton was founded in 1796 where four shallow streams meet and was named in honor of Gen. Jonathan Dayton. Some 200 years later, families still wander among the original buildings of one of the city's first communities, now known as the Oregon Historical District. The 12-block area along East Fifth Street between Wayne Avenue and Patterson Boulevard is home to antiques shops, lively restaurants and pubs, and a well-attended Christmas tour in December that spotlights the area's history and vintage homes. (For information call 937–223–0538.)

Dayton is better known as the home of almost 2,000 manufacturing plants and as the birthplace of the Wright brothers. Orville and Wilbur's original laboratory has been moved to Greenfield Village in Dearborn, Michigan, but Dayton visitors can still see Orville Wright's home in Oakwood at Harmon and Park Avenues as well as other Wright-related memorabilia in the city's museums and historic areas.

Recent renovations include Riverscape, located in the heart of downtown. Marked by a huge fountain that shoots water 200 feet into the air, it includes rowboat, canoe, and paddleboat rentals; summer laser shows; and an inventors' walk. In winter a junior hockey-size ice rink is the main attraction.

Carillon Historical Park (all ages) 🏛

1000 Carillon Boulevard; (937) 293–2841; www.carillonpark.org. Open Tuesday through Saturday from 9:30 A.M. to 5:00 P.M. and Sunday from noon to 5:00 P.M. $, children under three free.

Do your kids think Wilbur and Orville Wright make popcorn? Help their imaginations soar with a visit to the city's Carillon Historical Park. The *Wright Flyer III,* in which Orville and Wilbur taught themselves to fly, is one of the many treasures at this village-like sixty-five-acre outdoor museum of history, transportation, and invention. Start your tour at the Kettering Family Education Center, which features changing exhibits.

Besides the many aviation-related artifacts, there are antique autos, a fancy railroad car, and a replica of the Wright brothers' bicycle shop. Highlights include a 1905 Wright brothers' airplane, a 1930s print shop, and an 1896 schoolhouse. Dayton's oldest building, the 1796 Newcom Tavern, is also here. If you're hungry, check out Culps Cafe, modeled after downtown Dayton's Culps Cafeteria, a popular 1930s and 1940s eatery. The park is named for the stately fifty-bell carillon that towers over the grounds.

Dayton Aviation Heritage National Historic Park (ages 3 and up)

22 South Williams Street; (937) 225–7705; www.nps.gov/daav. Admission is free **to parts of the park (Wright Cycle Company Complex and Huffman Prairie); Aviation Center and Paul Laurence Dunbar State Memorial. $**

If your amateur aviators are interested in Wright landmarks, the National Park Service established eighty-six-acre Dayton Heritage National Historical Park to honor the Wrights' legacy and the work of their friend Paul Laurence Dunbar. A free guide to the park's historic buildings and the city's Aviation Trail is available. Four National Historic Landmarks and a National Historic District are within the park. Highlights include the Huffman Prairie Flying Field Interpretive Center, the Wright Cycle Company Complex, and the Paul Laurence Dunbar State Memorial. A new Junior Ranger program is designed for kids six to twelve. Booklets are available for $3.50 at the visitor center. The park celebrated its one-hundredth anniversary in 2003 as part of the celebration of the Wright brothers' first flight in December 1903.

Only in **Ohio**

Ohio has bragging rights to a number of superlatives. They include:

- The world's largest air and space museum (Dayton)
- The world's only rock and roll museum (Cleveland)
- Home of the first man on the Moon (Neil Armstrong; Wapakoneta)
- The world's largest Amish population (near Cleveland)
- America's largest arboretum (Holden Arboretum, Kirtland)
- The first museum built to house American art (Butler; Youngstown)

Amazing
Ohio Facts

The Dayton Air Show is the leading event of its kind in North America, drawing more than 250,000 people and 150 types of aircraft annually.

The Cincinnati/northern Kentucky area has had a long tradition in catering to kids. In 1905 Daniel Carter Beard founded the Sons of Daniel Boone here, which eventually evolved into the Boy Scouts of America.

Dayton Air Show (all ages)
(800) 848–3699 or www.airshowdayton.com for dates and information.

Ever seen a fire-breathing, four-story-tall, airplane-eating monster robot? Sights like this are commonplace at the spectacular Dayton Air Show, held each July at the city's international airport in Vandalia. An action-packed weekend of aviation adventures starts at 7:00 A.M. with thundering jets, incredible aerobatics, barnstormers, sky-divers, air racing, balloons, explosive pyrotechnics, and more. A newer offering is the kids' hangar, which has a sandbox, crafts, an aviation-themed gym, and roving celebrity autographs.

U.S. Air Force Museum (ages 4 and up)
Springfield Pike (444) at Gate 28B, Wright-Patterson Air Force Base; (937) 255–3286; www.wpafb.af.mil/museum. Open daily 9:00 A.M. to 5:00 P.M. Free. IMAX theater: adults $$, students $.

Hitch a ride on the back of a giant dragonfly, drift over Niagara Falls in a hot-air balloon, wing walk over the Grand Canyon, experience the last big San Francisco earthquake, or soar over the walls of a castle in France on a set of wings made only of feathers. The dynamics of natural and mechanical flight are the focus of the breathtaking IMAX theater at the U.S. Air Force Museum, the oldest and largest military-aviation museum in the world. The museum is recognized as one of sixty international museums that "change the way one sees the world," by the American Association of Museums. It was one of only two aviation museums and one of three domestic military museums so honored.

The 60 by 80-foot theater is like no other movie palace you've ever seen. The giant screen is as high as a six-story building and projects an image that's three times larger than a standard movie. The dynamic sound system is among the best modern technology has produced. This, in combination with a steeply inclined auditorium, gives your family the feeling of being in the middle of the action. Films change regularly and are screened seven days a week on the hour from 10:00 A.M. to 5:00 P.M.

But that's not all there is to experience at this incredible museum. Located on the Wright-Patterson Air Force Base about 5 miles northeast of downtown Dayton, the museum is also the most popular **free** attraction in the state. Some ten acres of outstanding exhibits span the history of flight from hot-air balloons to the B-1 bomber and attract some 1.6 million visitors each year.

Highlights include the famous British Sopwith Camel, a classic aircraft from World War I; one-of-a-kind planes including the North American XB-70 Valkyrie; an original Wright wind tunnel; and the original *Apollo 15* command module. If all this seems a little overwhelming to your kids, steer them toward the Discovery Hangar Five, an interactive exhibit that focuses on the hows and whys of flight and teaches children about the different types of airplanes, the parts of a plane, and how they work. Newer exhibits include the Wild Weasels of the Vietnam War and the relocated *Memphis Belle.*

Aullwood Audubon Center and Farm (all ages)

1000 Aullwood Road; (937) 890–7360; www.aullwood.center.audubon.org. Open Monday through Saturday from 9:00 A.M. to 5:00 P.M. and Sunday from 1:00 to 5:00 P.M. $

Perhaps the Wrights were inspired by the many wild birds that called the Dayton area home. Today the descendants of those birds are found in the Aullwood Audubon Center and Farm on Aullwood Road. This 350-acre wildlife refuge and educational farm lets your kids get up close and personal with more than 200 examples of animal, bird, and plant life. Five miles of trails meander through streams, woods, and meadows and make a hearty hike even for fit families. A hands-on nature center allows children to learn at their own pace or identify one of the center's many bird varieties. The new Birds, Flight, and The Wrights Trail features interpretive exhibits about the birds, insects, and bats that inspired the Wright brothers to uncover the mystery of flight.

Boonshoft Museum of Discovery (ages 2 and up)

2600 DeWeese Parkway; (937) 275–7431; www.boonshoftmuseum.org. Open 9:00 A.M. to 5:00 P.M. Monday through Friday, 11:00 A.M. to 5:00 P.M. Saturday, noon to 5:00 P.M. Sunday. Adults $$, children ages two to twelve $.

Your kids will be seeing stars at the innovative Carl D. Philips Space Theater, part of the Museum of Discovery. The Space Theater has a planetarium with a state-of-the-art Digistar system that guides visitors on computerized star treks throughout the universe.

During a visit your family will discover secrets of the natural world from across continents to your own backyard. Science Central includes a lab, theater, and three-story discovery tower. Eco-Trek offers reproductions of desert, woodland, tropical, and tidal-pool environments. You also can travel back in time to see the tools, jewelry, and other artifacts of the peoples that inhabited the Miami Valley 14,000 years ago. Explore an Egyptian tomb; peek into the rocky den of VanCleve, the museum's resident bobcat; or take a walk on the wild side during a visit to Wild Ohio, an indoor zoo that features more than fifty animals native to the Buckeye State in their own habitat.

Kids (and adults) interested in falcons should check out the falcon cam, which tracks Snowball and her mate, Mercury, in their downtown Dayton nest.

Dayton Art Institute (all ages)

456 Belmonte Park North; (937) 223–5277, (800) 296–4426; www.daytonartinstitute .org. Open Monday through Saturday from 10:00 A.M. to 4:00 P.M. and Thursday until 8:00 P.M. Admission is free.

Feel as if almost everything in Dayton is related to exploration of air and space? Come back to Earth with a visit to the Dayton Art Institute, where inspiration takes a more concrete form. This museum, which looks remarkably like an Italian villa and towers over the city on a nearby hill, is the Miami Valley's only fine-arts museum and has noteworthy examples of European painting and a stunning East Asian wing. Its holdings represent more than 10,000 objects spanning 5,000 years. Recent travelling exhibits have included everything from The Quest for Immortality: Treasures of Ancient Egypt to Diana: A Celebration.

Of special interest to families is the Experiencenter, where you can encourage your young van Goghs. This hands-on area—including more than twenty activities just for kids—prompts visitors to interact with art and experiment with the basic elements of line, pattern, color, texture, and shape.

Sunwatch Prehistoric Archaeological Park/Indian Village
(all ages)

2301 West River Road, off Interstate 75; (937) 268–8199; www.sunwatch.org. Open Tuesday through Saturday from 9:00 A.M. to 5:00 P.M. and Sunday from noon to 5:00 P.M. $, children under six free.

Most re-created historic villages in the state trace Ohio's roots to the colonial era or the nineteenth century. Sunwatch Village takes your family back a few moccasin-clad steps farther into the world of an 800-year-old Native American village.

Some 800 years ago, a group of Ohio's early farmers, now known as the Fort Ancient Indians, settled along the banks of the Great Miami River. The national landmark came dangerously close to becoming a sewage treatment plant in the 1980s. More than twenty years of excavation was completed before the village was constructed; today it consists of thatched huts surrounded by a stockade. In recognition of its significance, Sunwatch was designated a National Historic Landmark in 1990.

During a visit your kids will learn how to tell time based on an ancient, complex system of charting the sun; discover how archaeologists pieced together the fragments of their finds to create a rich and complex culture; and see how the village's ancient inhabitants used bone, skin, and stone to create beautiful and useful objects. Tours include the Big House, where Native American councils were held; and life-size dioramas that display unearthed artifacts. Special seasonal events celebrate planting and the harvest; the diversity of Native American culture and the annual homage to summer; and a weekend of traditional dancing, music, craft demonstrations, and more.

If you're lucky, your family will visit on Kids Dig Ohio Archaeology Day in June. The interpretive center is being improved until spring 2006, when it will reopen to the public.

Carriage Hill Metropark (ages 2 and up) 🐟🐌🐿🏠
East Shull Road; (937) 879–0461. Open Monday through Friday from 10:00 A.M. to 5:00 P.M. and Saturday and Sunday from 1:00 to 5:00 P.M. Admission by donation.

This large (1,000-acre) metropark includes a working historical farm as well as large woodland and meadow areas. The farm dates to about 1880 and lists a summer kitchen, smithy, woodshop, and barns among its restored buildings. A handy visitor center displays farm-related implements and has children's hands-on activities and audiovisual programs.

In season, the kitchen garden is planted with vegetables that are later harvested and preserved. Year-round activities include fishing, picnicking, hiking, and horseback riding. In autumn, popular events include hayrides, harvest events, and other special programs. Cross-country skiing, sledding, and ice skating are available in winter.

Wegerzyn Gardens Metropark (all ages) 🏛🍁
1301 East Siebenthaler Avenue; (937) 277–6545; www.metroparks.org. Open daily from 9:00 A.M. to 5:00 P.M. Free.

You'll enjoy the formal gardens featuring a variety of themes, including a charming children's area. Wetlands and the 350-foot boardwalk are family favorites.

Cox Arboretum & Gardens (all ages) 🚶🍁
6733 Springboro Pike Road; (937) 434–9005; www.metroparks.org. Open daily from 8:00 A.M. to dusk; visitor center 8:30 A.M. to 4:30 P.M. Monday through Friday, 1:00 to 4:00 P.M. Saturday and Sunday. Admission by donation.

An edible landscape garden, a butterfly house, and 1½ miles of nature trails are only a few of the family-friendly attractions at this fine arboretum and gardens near downtown, one of Dayton's twenty-five fine metropark facilities. The 175-acre preserve, off I–75 (exit 44), also has a water garden, shrub garden, a variety of plant collections, and an indoor visitor center that contains a reference library, an auditorium for special events, and seasonable art and plant exhibits.

Paul Laurence Dunbar State Memorial (ages 4 and up) 🏛

219 North Paul Laurence Dunbar Street; (937) 224–7061; www.ohiohistory.org/places/
dunbar. Open Wednesday through Saturday from 9:00 A.M. to 5:00 P.M. and Sunday from
12:30 to 5:00 P.M. in summer, weekends only otherwise. $; children under 6 free.

More recent—but no less fascinating—history is found at the Dunbar House, part of
Dayton Aviation Heritage National Historic Park. Think your kids are little geniuses?
Although born into a life of poverty, African-American poet Paul Laurence Dunbar
wrote his first poem at age six and recited publicly at age nine. He later edited the
school newspaper, wrote for various Dayton-area newspapers, and published his first
book of poetry at the ripe old age of twenty. He counted among his friends the
Wright brothers, Booker T. Washington, and Frederick Douglass.

Dunbar was the first African-American writer to gain acceptance in national and
international literary circles. He later moved to Washington, D.C., became a promi-
nent speaker about civil rights issues, and found fame, if not fortune. A longtime suf-
ferer of tuberculosis, he died at just thirty-three but continues to serve as inspiration
to millions today.

Dunbar's home in Dayton has been restored to appear as it did when he lived
there, including rooms furnished with his own possessions. On display are Dunbar's
bike, built by the Wright brothers; the desk and chair where he composed much of
his work; his collection of Native American art; and—the favorite of young male visitors—a ceremonial sword presented to Dunbar by President Teddy Roosevelt.

Where to Eat

The Barnsider, 5202 North Main Street;
(937) 277–1332. A local favorite, with a
casual atmosphere, a kids' menu, and a
menu that emphasizes steak and seafood.
$–$$

Caffé Anticoli, 8268 North Main Street;
(937) 890–0300. Run by the same family
for more than sixty-five years, with traditional Italian favorites and seafood entrees.
Pasta-pleasing kids' menu. $–$$

Where to Stay

Crowne Plaza, 33 East Fifth Street; (937)
224–0800. Centrally located, with an
indoor pool, on-site restaurant, and free
movies. $$

Doubletree Hotel & Suites, 11 South
Ludlow; (937) 461–4700. Handy, historic
downtown hotel with thirty-three spacious,
two-bedroom units perfect for families. $$

Holiday Inn North, 2301 Wagoner-Ford
Road; (937) 278–4871. Well-run chain hotel
with 231 rooms and a family fun center
with playground and indoor recreation
area. $$

For More Information

**Dayton/Montgomery County
Convention & Visitors Bureau,** (800)
221–8234 or (800) 221–8235 (outside
Ohio); www.daytoncvb.com.

Xenia

Blue Jacket Outdoor Drama 🎵 🍴

Call (937) 376–4358, (877) 465–BLUE (2583); www.bluejacketdrama.com. Shows are held nightly at 8:00 P.M. except Monday; tickets $$ to $$$. A dinner buffet and twice-daily backstage tours also are available.

The epic struggle between the Shawnee Indians who called this area home and the frontiersmen who arrived to claim it as their own provides plenty of exciting action at the *Blue Jacket* Outdoor Drama, held June through September at the 1,500-seat Caesar's Ford Park Amphitheater.

Blue Jacket is the true story of a white man adopted into the Shawnee Indian nation who in the late 1700s became their war chief. (Some historians and family claim he was actually a Shawnee, but this remains a less-popular account.) You'll share Blue Jacket's friendship with the warrior Caesar and their struggle to protect the Shawnee homeland against frontiersmen such as Daniel Boone and Simon Kenton.

The first performance was staged in 1982. More than fifty actors, a dozen horses, more than 1,000 costume pieces, and dazzling pyrotechnics and special effects are used to make this story come alive.

Where to Stay

Best Western Regency, 600 Little Main Street; (937) 372–9954. A small chain hotel, with just nineteen rooms, on a busy commercial strip. $

Holiday Inn Xenia, 300 Xenia Towne Square; (937) 372–9921. Centrally located hotel with eighty-eight rooms, patio dining in summer, and free morning coffee. $–$$

Kings Mills

Paramount Kings Island (all ages) 🎢

6300 Kings Island Drive; (513) 754–5700, (800) 288–0808; www.pki.com. Hours vary with the season. Call for current admission prices.

The 330-foot replica of the Eiffel Tower rising from the rolling hills of Ohio farmland not far from Cincinnati is disconcerting at first. Then you realize that this French fantasy is right at home among all of the others at this king of amusement parks in southern Ohio. A trip to Paris? *Bien sûr!* A ride into space on the starship *Enterprise*? Beam me up, Scotty. Anything seems possible here.

Each year Paramount Kings Island, the Midwest's largest theme park, tries to top itself with new shows and a new ride that's designed to be faster and scarier than the one introduced the year before. In 2001 the park introduced a three-and-a-half-acre

Nickelodeon area, with a kids' roller coaster, cartoon characters, a Slime Time Live! stage, and more. In 2002 the hot new ride was "Tomb Raider: The Ride," which plays off adventurous antics from the movie. The summer of 2003 saw the addition of Delirium, a thrilling, dropping, spinning, coaster-style ride that swings rocketing riders up in the air more than thirteen stories. The largest ride of its kind in the world, it is located in the park's Action Zone. More recently Paramount introduced the most elaborate collection of Nickelodeon-inspired rides in the world. Opening in spring 2006, the Nick universe includes eighteen new rides and brings to life characters and shows such as *Fairly Oddparents, Rugrats,* and *Jimmy Neutron.* It's no wonder the park has long been ranked "Best Kids Area in the World."

The king of this island, "The Beast," is now more than twenty years old. It's even listed in the *Guinness Book of World Records.* With 7,400 feet of track, the ominous Beast is the longest wooden roller coaster in the world. The ride lasts three minutes and forty seconds, with riders reaching a maximum speed of almost 65 miles per hour. Almost as frightening is the Vortex, which sends screaming riders through six hair-raising upside-down loops before bringing them to a crashing halt. (*Warning*: These roller coasters may be too stressful for young children.)

Want to keep your feet planted firmly on terra firma? No problem. Visitors who choose to skip the scream machines can get wet and wild at the thirty-acre water park. A family favorite, it includes sixteen water slides, including white-water rafting, and is **free** with park admission, unlike others in the Midwest. A new and improved model was introduced in 2004. The park also recently announced plans for another Great Wolf Lodge Indoor Water Park to open in Mason in late 2006.

Tiny thrill-seekers can meet their favorite cartoon characters and get a hug from Yogi or Scooby-Doo at a new location next door to Scooby-Doo and the Haunted Castle, a new family ride added in 2003. Or you can choose from more than one hundred other rides, many of them refreshingly tame. Paramount Kings Island has something for everyone. For the more traditional minded, Coney Mall has all the sights, sounds, and smells of an old-fashioned amusement park. The park is 24 miles north of Cincinnati. Two-day passes are available.

The Beach Waterpark (all ages) 🎟️🌊

2590 Waterpark Drive, Mason; (800) 886–7946, (513) 398–7946; www.thebeachwater park.com. Open daily from 10:00 A.M. to 9:00 P.M. June through August 17; 10:00 A.M. to 7:00 P.M. in September. Call (800) 398–SWIM (7946) for ticket prices and other information.

Across from Kings Island is the Midwest's largest water park, also known as The Beach. Endless summer is the attraction here, where your family can catch a real wave at the Thunder Beach wave pool, float along the Lazy Miami River on a 1½-mile ride with a riverboat motif, or brave the Twilight Zoom, a double-tube water slide that ends with an exciting splashdown.

Amazing
Ohio Facts

The *New York Times*—which seldom writes much about the Midwest—named The Beach one of America's ten best water parks.

Afterward, boogie to Jamaican tunes played by a live reggae band, cavort on more than thirty water slides and attractions, or relax on 40,000 sprawling square feet of beach—more than enough for a few impressive sand castles. With thirty-five acres and two million gallons of wild waves, the park is the perfect wild and watery family escape. There's even Splash Mountain for the little squirts, with lots of warm water and pint-size play areas.

New attractions include Volcanic Panic; Aztec Adventure; the only water coaster in the Midwest, the 85-foot, 60-mile-per-hour Bonzai slide; and Twilight Zoom, a lights-out superslide.

Where to Stay

There's no lack of places to stay around Kings Island and in nearby Mason. There are also many options in neighboring Cincinnati. A few good bets are:

Comfort Suites Kings Island, 5457 Kings Center Drive; (513) 336–9000. This newer hotel has spacious rooms, an indoor pool, **free** breakfast, and a convenient guest laundry. $$

Hampton Inn Kings Island, 5323 Beach Boulevard; (513) 459–8900. Economy-minded but comfortable, with ninety units, laundry, and small pool. $

Holiday Inn Express Kings Island, 5589 Kings Mills; (513) 398–8075. Offerings include 194 rooms, package rates, twenty-four-hour restaurant, and nicely planned public areas; across from park. $$

Lebanon

Settled in 1796 and rich in history, Lebanon is home to the state's oldest inn and restaurant, as well as more than forty charming antiques and specialty shops.

The Golden Lamb (ages 3 and up) 🏛 🍴 🛏

27 South Broadway; (513) 932–5065; www.goldenlamb.com. $$–$$$.

The Golden Lamb, which dates to 1803, has hosted ten U.S. presidents and various worldwide luminaries. George Washington may not have slept here, but you can put your feet up in the same room (and in some cases, the same bed) where Charles

Dickens or Samuel Clemens (Mark Twain) laid their hallowed heads. The inn's eighteen rooms are named for the famous people who slept there. (Interestingly enough, Dickens was less than complimentary when he visited the United States in 1842; only later did innkeeper Calvin Bradley discover that the "small, rather disagreeable man" who eloquently bellowed his less than favorable opinions about America to anyone who would listen was the illustrious author of *A Christmas Carol* and other classics.)

Even if you choose not to stay in one of the rooms, your family can absorb a little of the area's rich history with a meal in one of the famous dining rooms. There are four public and five private dining areas. The specialty in each is all-American—from Yankee pot roast and tasty turkey with mashed potatoes to old-fashioned apple pie and other home-baked desserts. On Sunday local families crowd the tables to celebrate birthdays and anniversaries, so reservations are a good idea.

Unoccupied rooms are always open for inspection. While there, head up to the fourth floor, where you can check out a series of guest rooms decorated with Shaker and period furnishings—one is known as Sarah's Room and was furnished for Sarah Stubbs, who lived at the inn as a child. The room is a little girl's dream, complete with a nostalgic collection of furniture and toys that will have any child itching to step inside.

If you saved room for dessert, a good place to have it is the Village Ice-Cream Parlor across the street. This ice-cream parlor is so classic that even Hollywood has discovered it: It had a supporting role in both *Harper Valley P.T.A.* with Barbara Eden and the more recent film *Milk Money,* with Ed Harris and Melanie Griffith. With wire chairs, ceiling fans, and specialties that include a Shaker Sundae (vanilla, chocolate, and strawberry ice cream topped with chocolate, butterscotch, and strawberry syrups, cherries, and nuts), it'll have you dieting for weeks afterward.

For More Information

Warren County Convention and Visitors Bureau, (800) 791–4386, (513) 695–1138; www.ohio4fun.org.

Oregonia

Fort Ancient State Memorial (all ages) 🏛 🐛 🚻 🚗

6123 Highway 350; (513) 932–4421, (800) 283–8904; www.ohiohistory.org. Hours vary by season. $ per car.

Southwest of Lebanon, the awesome earthworks at Fort Ancient State Memorial are an important North American archaeological site. On a bluff rising some 240 feet above the Little Miami River, the prehistoric Hopewell Indians (circa 100 B.C. to A.D.

Amazing
Ohio Facts

Fort Ancient, Ohio's first state park, was later reclassified as a state memorial and put under the jurisdiction of the Ohio Historical Society. Visit the society's Web site at www.ohiohistory.org for more information on sites and future expansion plans.

500) constructed more than 3½ miles of earth and stone walls now known as Fort Ancient. The one-hundred acre enclosure, one of the nation's finest examples of a Hopewell hilltop community, is now a National Historic Landmark.

While there you may see kids of all ages sifting through the dirt of a mock archaeological site as part of the site's popular Digging the Past program. It is believed that the site was used both for defense and as a gathering place for social and religious ceremonies.

Families can learn about both groups at the newly expanded $3.5 million on-site museum, which contains archaeological finds and more. Exhibits here explore Hopewell and Fort Ancient artifacts and culture. New displays include a re-created prehistoric Native American garden; a resource center with books, articles, and records; and more than 9,000 feet of expanded exhibit space.

Afterward, pull on your hiking boots and explore the Earthworks Trail, which stretches for about a mile and offers two scenic overlooks with clear views of the earthworks. There's also a comfortable picnic area, perfect for an open-air snack or meal.

Waynesville

This tiny town—home to the first Stetson hat and to more than thirty-five tempting antiques shops, earning it the nickname "Antiques Capital of the Midwest"—attracts thousands of revelers to the area during two annual festivals. Each year it pays homage to an unlikely pair: cabbages and kings.

Ohio Renaissance Festival (all ages)
Held annually from late August through mid-October in nearby Harveysburg. For information call (513) 897–7000; www.renfestival.com. $$ to $$$

Ever seen the movie *Brigadoon*? Willy-Nilly-on-the-Wash, although less melodic, is a town, like Brigadoon, that only exists for a short time. On weekends from late August through mid-October, the sixteenth-century town appears magically on more than thirty acres just east of downtown on Highway 73 (technically in Harveysburg). At the annual Ohio Renaissance Festival your kids can speak with Shakespeare, juggle with a jester, even crack open a dragon egg.

More than 150 costumed peasants, pirates, merchants, and royalty (even a few serfs and fools) bring the era to life. There's a joust three times daily, complete with clanking armor and flying pennants. Here your family can wander among the wares of more than 130 merchants selling everything from shields to stone sculpture, dance the jig around the maypole, learn the art of swordplay and chivalry, and afterward sample the hearty food and drink of the age at one of many food stands. For even more fun, schedule a visit during one of the special theme weekends in September and October, when the classic tale of Robin Hood comes alive or the Queen celebrates her birthday, or when games of skill challenge visitors and villagers at the Highland Games. Huzzah!

Caesar Creek State Park (all ages)

8570 East Highway 73 (Clarksville Road); (513) 897–3055; www.dnr.state.oh.us/parks/ parks/caesarck.

Recreational fun on a 2,800-acre lake, including swimming, fishing, and more, attracts families. There's also a nature preserve and wildlife area, as well as a visitor center filled with fossils and Native American artifacts. On the premises is Pioneer Village, a restored nineteenth-century village with a Quaker meetinghouse and an 1807 founder's home.

Sauerkraut Festival (all ages)

For information call the Waynesville Chamber of Commerce at (513) 897–8855; www .sauerkrautfestival.com. Free.

Like your fun on the sour side? Pucker up and chow down during the two-day Ohio Sauerkraut Festival, held each year the second full weekend in October. You may have heard of sauerkraut on a hot dog, but you'll be amazed at all the other culinary uses for this cabbage creation.

Ever try sauerkraut fudge? How 'bout sauerkraut pizza? Here's your chance. Even doughnuts and cream pies get a dollop of kraut at the booths that line Main Street during this festive event, which began in 1972. Strangely enough, Waynesville has no special ties to this food specialty: The festival began because a local businessman who wanted to start up a local fall festival had sauerkraut for lunch.

Besides sampling sauerkraut, your family can browse and buy from the arts and crafts of more than 400 craftspeople who line the street, enjoy continuous entertain-ment, and just people-watch among the more than 250,000 kraut cravers of all ages who flock to this charming town.

For More Information

Waynesville Area Chamber of Commerce, (513) 897–8855 or www.waynesvilleohio.com.

Jeffersonville

Prime Outlets at Jeffersonville (ages 5 and up) 🔒
8000 Factory Shops Boulevard; (800) 746–7644, (740) 948–9090; www.primeoutlets .com. **Open Monday through Saturday from 10:00 A.M. to 9:00 P.M. and Sunday from 11:00 A.M. to 6:00 P.M.**

Outlet shopping has become an American obsession, with many people sharing their savvy secrets with friends. On weekends and at Christmas, this place can start to look like Grand Central Station.

If your family has been bitten by the bug, a good place to bag great bargains is the centrally located Prime Outlets at Jeffersonville, which is about thirty-five minutes from Dayton, thirty-five minutes from Columbus, and fifty minutes from Cincinnati. The intersection of Interstate 71 and U.S. Highway 35 is the location of the state's largest outlet mall, where you'll find a parking lot full of cars and stores full of bargains.

You'll save 25 to 70 percent off retail prices at stores that include Baby Guess/Guess Kids, for up-to-date school fashions; the Springmaid/Wamsutta store, for towels and sheets; and The Nature Company, for great kids' toys with a geological or natural bent. More toys at bargain prices can be found at the Toy Warehouse, a good place to set Dad and the kids free while Mom shops.

None of those appeal to you? There are more than seventy-five stores in a covered, villagelike setting, as well as an outdoor playground for when the kids (or you) want to blow off a little steam.

America's **Most Haunted**

Waynesville is known for its antiques shops and also for its ghosts. The town's Main Street has been dubbed "America's Most Haunted." Visit in October and you can sign on for a Not So Dearly Departed tour that takes in the historic (and haunted!) Hammel House Inn and Lebanon's Pioneer Cemetery, eternal resting place of four sisters who, according to *Ripley's Believe It or Not*, were killed simultaneously by a bolt of lightning that hit their farmhouse— even though they were in different rooms.

Where to Stay

Amerihost Inn, 11431 Allen Road Northwest; (614) 948–2104 or 10160 Carr Road Northwest; (740) 426–6400. Two handy locations with sixty rooms near outlet mall; indoor pool and restaurants nearby. **Free** breakfast and newspaper. $

Cincinnati

Winston Churchill once called Cincinnati "the most beautiful of America's inland cities." This big city, perched high on the bluffs of the Ohio River, is known for its small-town charm. It also has a vibrant and exciting downtown, with a 20-block elevated skywalk system connecting department stores, specialty shops, restaurants, hotels, and even a museum. It's also as far south as you can go in the state without hitting the bluegrass of Kentucky, located just across the river.

Your family is sure to agree with Churchill after a visit to the Queen City (so named because of its riverboat "queens" history). From the first professional fire department (and a museum honoring it) to the equally fiery and famous Skyline Chili, known 'round the world, this is one hot and happenin' city.

A good place to get a grip on the city's psyche is downtown's Fountain Square, where the *Genius of Water* sculpture atop the Tyler Davidson Fountain surveys a broad, open plaza. In sunny weather you'll find shoppers and businesspeople "brown-bagging" it on the square or enjoying some famous chili while being entertained by performances on the open-air pavilion stage. The plaza is also home to the Cincy Shop, where your family can find maps, books, guides, and virtually any Cincinnati-related item your hearts could desire.

For a great introduction to the city, check out the visitor center, which opened in the summer of 2001. The glass-enclosed, 3,300-square-foot facility showcases area attractions, history, and culture and is located in the Fifth Third Center.

Parky's Farm (all ages) 🐘 🎠
10073 Daly Road; (513) 521–3276; www.hamiltoncountyparks.org.
Located in Winton Woods, one of Hamilton County's fine suburban Cincinnati parks, this one-hundred-acre farm is a family favorite. Besides a two-story indoor playground that's popular year-round, there's a working windmill, a barn filled with friendly animals, antique farm equipment, and pony rides for the little ones.

Sharon Woods Village (all ages) 🏛
11450 Lebanon Road, Sharon Woods Park; (513) 563–4513; www.hamiltoncountyparks .org. Open 10:00 A.M. to 4:00 P.M. Wednesday through Friday and 1:00 to 5:00 P.M. on weekends.

Arranged to depict pioneer life in the early nineteenth century, this reconstructed village, set on 750 acres in a county park, recently celebrated its seventy-fifth anniversary. It includes interpreters in period costumes, seasonal events, and regular Civil War reenactments. There are also ten restored buildings, including a train station, a doctor's office, and a log home filled with period furnishings, antique household items, and other antiques.

Harriet Beecher Stowe House (ages 5 and up)

2950 Gilbert Avenue; (513) 632–5120; www.ohiohistory.org. Open Tuesday and Wednesday from 10:00 A.M. to 2:00 P.M. Free.

Older children and history buffs love exploring the Cincinnati home of author Harriet Beecher Stowe, whose most famous book, *Uncle Tom's Cabin*, brought the evils of slavery to the attention of a wider world. Exhibits describe the Beecher family, the nineteenth-century abolitionist movement, and the history of African Americans in America.

Cincinnati Nature Center (ages 3 and up)

4949 Tealtown Road; (513) 831–1711; www.cincynature.org. Open Monday through Saturday from 9:00 A.M. to 5:00 P.M. and Sunday from 1:00 to 5:00 P.M. $

Looking to escape the city for a while? Highlights of this 790-acre preserve include nature trails covering more than 14 miles, an indoor nature center with displays and a fascinating bird-watching area, and a 534-acre working cattle farm that is open only during special events. In summer, the center is the site of popular Cincy Nature Camps for kids ages three through thirteen.

Eden Park (all ages)

Other great views of the city can be had at one of the scenic overlooks in Eden Park, part of the stylish, high-rent Mount Adams neighborhood. When the skyscrapers and the bustle get to be too much, city residents of all ages retreat to this well-used greensward. This sprawling park boasts many of Cincy's most popular attractions, including its renowned art museum, two professional theaters, and miles and miles of trails perfect for walking, hiking, biking, or in-line skating (just remember to wear pads; the hills can be steep!).

Cincinnati Art Museum (ages 2 and up)

953 Eden Park Drive; (513) 721–ARTS (2787); www.cincinnatiartmuseum.org. Open Tuesday through Sunday from 11:00 A.M. to 5:00 P.M. $, free for children under eighteen.

If you prefer, your family can choose a little slower pace with a stroll around the eighty-eight galleries of the Cincinnati Art Museum. This was the first museum west of the Alleghenies built to be a museum; today its graceful halls house art dating back some 5,000 years. Founded in 1881, the museum opened to world acclaim and was heralded as "The Art Palace of the West."

Not one to rest on its laurels, the museum recently completed the most extensive renovation in its more than one-hundred-year history. Today the collection and the museum's hilltop location still enchant visitors of all ages. In 2004, the museum purchased *Fog at Guernsey* by Renoir, its most expensive acquisition ever.

The medieval arms and armor—especially the sharp-edge poleaxes—look as menacing as they were intended to, but kids love them. They also love the old musical instruments, the huge untitled mural by Joan Miró (it originally hung in the restaurant of the city's Terrace Plaza Hotel and was later given to the museum), and the colorful *Red Rooster* by Marc Chagall. Mary Cassatt's poignant *Mother and Child* from 1889 will leave you wistful for your children's babyhood.

Steering wheels, hubcaps, refrigerator doors, ancient television cabinets, radio tubes—they're all art up in the contemporary galleries, where kids will be mesmerized by Korean sculptor Nam June Paik's futuristic robot entitled *Powel Crosley Jr.* The whimsical work pays homage to the television age and was commissioned by the museum in honor of Crosley, a father of modern telecommunications and onetime owner of the Cincinnati Reds. Baseball fans flock to Andy Warhol's baseball card–style tribute to Cincinnati Reds great Pete Rose.

Other museum favorites include six paintings of Native Americans and settlers by artist Henry Farny, works by local artist Frank Duveneck (including his most famous, *Whistling Boy,* which may have your kids puckering up and attempting a tune while you stand in front of it. Interestingly enough, research has shown that the boy isn't quite as innocent as he appears: He's really smoking, not whistling), and the extensive collection of Cincinnati-made Rookwood pottery. From ancient Egyptian to the more modern Expressionist school, there's something here for art lovers of all ages and interests.

There's also a monthly special program, For Curious Kids, which explores the wonders of the permanent collection and encourages creative thinking.

Cycling **Cincinnati**

The Little Miami Scenic Trail, Ohio's longest paved trail, stretches from the Queen City's northern suburbs past quiet countryside, historic sites, and charming country towns. Portions of the trail cut through the cliffs and woods of the Little Miami Scenic State Park. There are plenty of places in town to rent equipment if your family didn't bring its own. For more information contact Caesar Creek State Park, which manages it, at (513) 897–3055.

Irwin M. Krohn Conservatory (all ages)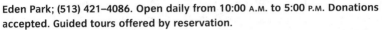
Eden Park; (513) 421–4086. Open daily from 10:00 A.M. to 5:00 P.M. Donations accepted. Guided tours offered by reservation.

Not far away, also in Eden Park, is the Krohn Conservatory, one of the nation's largest public greenhouses. Here your little green thumbs can adventure into the exotic world of tropical and desert plants and learn about horticulture firsthand. Wander through a tropical rain forest, walk under a spectacular 20-foot waterfall, or dry out in the desert greenhouse filled with prickly cacti and fabulous, delicate orchids. All of Cincy gathers for the seasonal events, which include festive holiday floral shows and an annual Butterfly Show, a family favorite.

Mount Adams

The neighborhood known as Mount Adams is also one of the city's liveliest. It's often compared to San Francisco, as much for its annoying one-way streets as its breathtaking hilltop views. Here you'll find narrow rowhouses, most restored to their former nineteenth-century glory, as well as funky shops and interesting restaurants.

Rookwood Pottery Restaurant (ages 3 and up)
1077 Celestial Street; (513) 721–5456.

Among the most interesting attractions in Mount Adams is the Rookwood Pottery Restaurant, housed in the former pottery of the same name. The restaurant over-looks Krohn Conservatory and the art museum. Rookwood, active from around the beginning of the twentieth century through the 1930s, is known for its intricate glazes and beautiful designs. It is highly prized by today's collectors.

Your kids will love the chance to sit inside one of the three huge brick kilns (which once reached thousands of degrees) while dining on the burgers voted the best in the city by *Cincinnati* magazine. (Like almost every other restaurant in the city, it also boasts its own brand of chili.) Vintage photographs, original pieces of pottery, and a great make-your-own sundae bar add to the ambience.

Playhouse in the Park (ages 5 and up)
962 Mount Adams Circle in Eden Park; (513) 345–2247, (800) 582–3208; www.cincy play.com for tickets and information.

Not far from the restaurant is the Cincinnati Playhouse in the Park, one of the city's intimate theaters. With a little more than 600 seats in the Circular Theater and 230 in the Shelterhouse Theater, it's known for offering unusual plays and family favorites. The Next Generation Series specializes in cutting-edge kids' theater. Recent offerings have included *Cat on a Hot Tin Roof* and *Love, Janis*. There's also a great view of the city from the parking lot, as well as a few well-used picnic tables that are perfect for a relaxing snack or meal.

Cincinnati Fire Museum (ages 2 and up) 🏛

315 West Court Street; (513) 621–5553; www.cincyfiremuseum.com. Open weekdays from 10:00 A.M. to 4:00 P.M. and weekends from noon to 4:00 P.M. $

Have your kids ever wanted to slide down a fire pole? They'll get their chance at the Cincinnati Fire Museum, a restored 1907 fire station where they also can test their strength and endurance by having a go at a replica of a hand-pumped engine. The city is known for being the site of the nation's first professional fire department—founded in the 1850s—and this museum touches on topics from bucket brigades to fire prevention in a way that's both educational and entertaining. There's even a wooden fire hose.

Museum Center at Cincinnati Union Terminal (all ages) 🏛

1301 Western Avenue; (800) 733–2077 for all museums or (513) 287–7000; www.cincy museum.org. Open Monday through Saturday from 10:00 A.M. to 5:00 P.M. and Sunday from 11:00 A.M. to 6:00 P.M. OMNIMAX shows are presented Monday through Friday beginning at 1:00 P.M. and Saturday and Sunday beginning at 11:00 A.M. $$; combination tickets are available and prices vary, $$$–$$$$.

Some cities choose to honor their past by tearing it down piece by piece in the name of progress. This is not so in preservation-minded Cincinnati, which, when faced with an unused Art Deco train station the size of fourteen football fields, decided to turn it into not one but four fantastic museums and an OMNIMAX theater.

Union Terminal was built in 1933 and once hosted up to 216 trains and 34,000 people daily. It closed in 1972, victim of America's love affair with the automobile. Now restored to its original grandeur, it stands as one of the country's most spectacular remaining examples of streamlined Art Deco architecture, with a magnificent soaring rotunda filled with murals and distinctive details.

Today this extraordinary cultural center on Western Avenue is a prime example of adaptive reuse. Inside the bright, soaring space—it covers 500,000 square feet—you'll find four family favorites: the Cincinnati History Museum, the Cincinnati Museum of Natural History and Science, the Robert D. Lindner Family OMNIMAX Theater, and the Cinergy Children's Museum of Cincinnati. They're known collectively as the Museum Center at Cincinnati Union Terminal.

Other Museum Center attractions include the Art Collection of the Cincinnati Public Schools, with ninety-seven paintings by nineteenth- and twentieth-century local artists; the Arts Consortium, with a changing art exhibit gallery and a high-tech journey though Cincy's Black history; and the Newsreel Theater, which shows World War II newsreels and is **free** to the public. Train lovers of all ages can experience the romance of the rails with a visit to the Radio Control Tower, originally used for train traffic control. Now restored by the Cincinnati Railroad Club, it's open Saturday from 10:00 A.M. to 4:00 P.M. and Tuesday and Thursday from 8:00 A.M. to 11:00 P.M.

Cincinnati History Museum (all ages)
Museum Center.

For an overview of the city's long and lively history, check out the Cincinnati History Museum first. Here your family can trace the Queen City's development from frontier river town to modern metropolis. Costumed interpreters escort you and your kids on a journey through time, from a frontier cabin to a 1940s-era gas station. Cincinnati: From Settlement to 1860 chronicles the city's founding and the often demanding pioneer lifestyle. Visit a settler's cabin and experience the rousing drum rolls and battle cries at Fort Washington.

As you move through the re-created streets of nineteenth-century Cincy, you'll hear boosters praise the city's past and future. Your kids will love the chance to learn about the area's agricultural products by moving wooden boats along a 50-foot model of the Miami and Erie Canals. River life is also the spotlight in the La Belle Riviere section, where your gang can board an old-fashioned flatboat (a plaque nearby calls it the "moving van of the frontier"), talk to a "real" pioneer family, and watch lively programs on river life.

The river and the historical role it played in city history are also chronicled in Queen City of the West, where you can imagine the thrill of a steamboat ride as you step on board a 94-foot side-wheel steamboat or stroll along an entire block of nineteenth-century shops. The modern era is represented by Cincinnati Goes to War. Spark young imaginations with a visit to a full-size gas station from the era and an authentic World War II broadcast studio. Kids even can climb aboard an original 1923 trolley that was used in the city until 1951 and take an imaginary ride through the

Cincinnati **Chili**

Don't leave Cincinnati without tasting its world-famous chili, served on almost every street corner. The Queen City has more chili joints than any other place in the world. Camp Washington Chili, open twenty-four hours, was even immortalized in a song and featured on national network news.

Cincinnati chili parlors such as Skyline and Gold Star, along with a number of independent local shops, dispense gallons of secret-recipe chili spiked with cinnamon and allspice (the spices are due to the chili's Greek origins). Cincy chili is unlike any other you've tasted. It's served three-way (ladled over spaghetti on a small platter and topped with mild cheddar cheese), four-way (add kidney beans or chopped onions), or five-way (add both). Oyster crackers are served on the side. The hot stuff even has its own festival, held downtown along West Court Street for two days at the end of September.

streets of vintage Cincy. A new exhibit is Cincinnati in Motion, a 164th-scale replica of the city as it looked in 1940.

The museum frequently hosts special family-style exhibits. Past favorites have included a display revolving around the role of the circus in American history (complete with **free** popcorn, face painting, and a huge miniature circus under the big top); a recent exhibit traced the influence of *Star Trek* on American culture.

Cincinnati Museum of Natural History and Science (all ages) 🖼
Museum Center.

Just steps away, the Cincinnati Museum of Natural History and Science captivates visitors of all ages. There's a special emphasis here on the natural and geological history of the Ohio Valley. Don't be surprised if the guides seem young: The museum's innovative Lab Rats program turns high school students into knowledgeable guides who perform scientific demonstrations and answer visitors' questions.

First stop: the Ice Age. Travel back 19,000 years in time to an era when ice covered the Ohio Valley. Walk through a mock glacier (better bring a sweater!) and feel the spine-tingling chill of living in a time when one-ton ground sloths and saber-toothed tigers roamed Earth. Afterward, go underground and navigate the narrow twists and turns in The Cavern, a simulated Kentucky limestone cave, complete with underground waterfalls, streams, fossils, and even a live bat colony (safely contained behind glass, of course).

Are your preschoolers bored with Barney? Let them experience the real thing in Dinosaur Hall, where interactive games and puzzles surround a dino exhibit and where they can have a hand at digging up a dinosaur bone using brushes and archaeological tools. A display extolling the virtues of recycling shows the incredible amount of garbage an average family of four uses in a week, as well as innovative and easy ways to reduce it.

Finally, turn the kids loose in the Children's Discovery Center, with two major hands-on areas. All About You teaches kids about the inner workings of the body; Pathways to Change lets them travel through time to learn how people through the ages have changed and adapted to their environment. Here they can brush a huge set of teeth, play Captain Digesto pinball (it traces the path food takes through the digestive system), and pretend to be a doctor or dentist in the kid-size offices.

Robert D. Lindner Family OMNIMAX Theater (ages 3 and up) 🎵
Museum Center; call (800) 733–2077 for shows and times. Adults $$, children ages three to twelve $.

Don't leave Museum Center without stopping at the OMNIMAX theater, which takes movies to new heights. There's no popcorn, but your local multiplex will pale in comparison to this five-story, 72-foot-wide domed screen.

This spectacular facility—the only such theater in the region—wraps your family in a hypersensory experience. Special technology enables you to experience every scene and motion with gut-wrenching, eye-popping clarity. The camera lets you zoom through dramatic, panoramic settings around the world and beyond from the comfort of your seat.

Movies change frequently. Past films have explored man's *Destiny in Space*, the natural wonders of *Yellowstone*, and even have gone *To the Max* with the Rolling Stones.

Cinergy Children's Museum of Cincinnati (all ages)

Museum Center; (513) 287–7000; www.cincymuseum.org. Open Wednesday, Thursday, and Sunday from noon to 5:00 P.M.; Friday from noon to 8:00 P.M.; and Saturday from 10:00 A.M. to 5:00 P.M. Age six to adult $$, kids five and younger $.

More fun tailored to small fry can be had at the Cinergy Children's Museum of Cincinnati, a newer and very welcome addition to the city's museum scene. Just a youngster at seven years old, the 30,000-square-foot museum has already attracted a loyal following of local and out-of-town kids and their parents.

Now located in the Museum Center at Cincinnati Union Terminal, the brightly colored $7.5 million space is guarded by a huge yellow, purple, and blue dragon that hangs playfully over the entrance. Don't let him deter you, however.

Once inside, you'll have a hard time holding on to the kids, who will be tempted to run off on their own to try the more than 200 hands-on activities spread out over three floors. The museum ranks among the top children's museums in the country. Designed for infants through age ten, it includes a variety of themed areas. Little Sprouts helps would-be farmers learn to weigh and price veggies. Kid's Town lets them deliver food to a neighborhood grocery or local restaurant. Not far away is The Woods, filled with caves, logs, a tree house, and a rope bridge; and Water Works, inspired by the city's watery location, which lets kids design boats and sail them. Other favorites include Little Sprouts Farm and Energy Zone.

Rookwood Ice Cream Parlor (all ages)

Museum Center.

Feeling hungry? Chow down on chili or refuel with a sweet treat in the Rookwood Ice Cream Parlor, with glowing walls and floors of authentic area-made Rookwood tile. Afterward stop and shop. Three Museum Center shops— the Collector's Shop at the Cincinnati Museum of Natural History and Science, and the Children's Shop and the Heritage Shop at the Cincinnati History Museum—sell gifts and goods that make great souvenirs of your visit.

Bicentennial Commons at Sawyer Point (all ages) (👥) (👫) (🌊)

After heating up with some chili (it's popular any time of year), cool down and get some fresh air at the Bicentennial Commons at Sawyer Point, one of the city's newest and most beloved parks. Built in honor of the city's bicentennial, it skirts the river and boasts an impressive roster of recreation facilities and scenic overlooks. When entering, look up to see the *Cincinnati Gateway Sculpture,* a whimsical, three-dimensional work that pays homage to the city's history. Interestingly, the sculpture was also quite controversial. Many residents were offended by the bronze winged pigs—a reference to the city's onetime nickname "Porkopolis" because of its pork industry—but many loved them, and today they stand as a playful reminder to residents not to take themselves too seriously.

While there, why not take a turn at the 21,000-square-foot roller-skating pavilion, a favorite of the city's in-line enthusiasts; join in a game of sand volleyball; or just wander along the 4-mile Riverwalk, where you can trace the city's time line and enjoy the great views of the Kentucky antebellum mansions across the way. A fishing pier encourages anglers of all ages to try their luck.

Riverfest/**Kids Fest**

Sawyer Point and the riverfront are also the location of the popular Riverfest, held each year during the first weekend in September. The region's largest Labor Day celebration is the site of its famous fireworks and other family events, including the annual Rubber Duck Regatta.

Each year during Riverfest up to 40,000 rubber ducks "dive" into the Ohio River at the L&N Bridge to power paddle in heated competition toward a finish line located at the *Showboat Majestic.* Proceeds benefit a local food bank. Anyone can enter—you just have to "adopt" a duck. Past prizes have included a Toyota truck, airline tickets, a Caribbean cruise, and family computer systems. If you're not interested in adoption, watching can be just as much fun.

Also celebrated here is the Kids Fest, the largest **free,** one-day children's event in the country. With more than one hundred activities—including face painting, games, and continuous entertainment—it's a sure hit each June and is sponsored by the city's Recreation Commission. For more festival information call the city's Convention & Visitors Bureau at (800) 543–2613 or visit the city's parks and recreation office Web site at www.cincyrec.org.

Newport Aquarium (all ages) 🐘

1 Aquarium Way, Newport, KY; (859) 261–7444; www.newportaquarium.com. Open 10:00 A.M. to 6:00 P.M. daily. Adults $$$, children ages three to twelve $$.

Cross the river into Kentucky and you'll discover this respected aquarium and local favorite. With more than 11,000 creatures in sixty exhibits, there's something for everyone. Themed areas include Rivers of the World, The Shore Gallery, even The Bizarre and Beautiful (my kids' favorite). There's also an area called The Dangerous and the Deadly and a simulated Ohio River Bank.

A newer favorite is Guardians of the Deep: A Shark Encounter, which explores the secret life of these awe-inspiring creatures. Here you can see the only Shark Ray in existence and watch divers feed "Sweet Pea" by hand. Kids can become young biologists as they touch shark teeth and skin, even walk through an 85-foot shark tunnel surrounded by the majestic fish. An expansion, completed in 2005, increased the aquarium's size by 25 percent.

Cincinnati Reds (ages 3 and up) ⚾

For ticket information call (800) 829–5353 outside Cincinnati, (513) 421–4510 in town; www.cincinnatireds.com.

Every kid in Cincinnati grows up wanting to play baseball for the Reds. Even if you're not interested in baseball, you probably know that the team has played in nine World Series (and won five of them) and has sent thirty-one players to the Baseball Hall of Fame. To many locals, Cincinnati and baseball go together like bacon and eggs.

It's not just that the Queen City had the first professional baseball team in the United States (it was founded in 1869). The city has been crazy about baseball since another Cincinnati resident, President William Howard Taft, threw out the first pitch in a ball game in Washington, D.C., and created a new American pastime (some would say obsession).

Baseball mania begins in April, when the Reds play their first game, and lasts through the end of the season. Between bites of a famous ballpark hot dog, you may even find yourselves hollering "Let's Go Reds" with everyone else.

The team's new home, the Great American Ballpark, debuted in 2003. The $290 million ballpark has quickly become a fans' favorite.

Showboat Majestic (ages 5 and up) 🎵 ⛵

Docked at Public Landing at the foot of Broadway at 435 East Mehring Way. Call (513) 241–6550 for ticket information.

Another view of the city skyline is available on one of the many nostalgic riverboats docked on the river. Take in a musical, comedy, or dramatic revue on the *Showboat Majestic*, the last of the original floating theaters. First launched in 1923, her builder, owner and actor Thomas Jefferson Reynolds, raised eleven children on board while entertaining at countless river towns in the era before malls and multiscreen cinemas. Today the *Majestic* features great shows from April through October on board this National Historic Landmark.

Steamboatin' **Cincinnati**

The first paddle wheeler churned up the Ohio River in 1811 and forever changed the course of American history. Steamboating vacations, steeped in adventure, romance, and history, are a legacy of nineteenth-century America and a reminder of a more gracious era.

The Queen City is one of the many colorful ports visited by the *Mississippi Queen*, the *Delta Queen*, and the *American Queen*, launched in 1995. These overnight paddle-wheel steamboats are the last to ply our nation's rivers. America's inland rivers, an area known as "Mark Twain's America," is the setting for three- to sixteen-night cruises.

On board, the sounds of a calliope—a mighty steam-and-iron piano—fill the area as the ship gets under way. Inside, guests feast on regional specialties, including Mississippi mud pie, better known as "heaven on a plate." Afterward, the rhythms of a ragtime piano and a strumming banjo (along with a few impromptu sing-alongs) keep the atmosphere lively.

The next day you can choose to explore a friendly port en route or simply relax on board. Kids enjoy tours of the ship's engine room and the pilothouse or a chance to try out the fancy calliope. For added fun, join the ships during one of their theme cruises, which include everything from all-American baseball and Civil War cruises to old-fashioned country Christmas cruises.

Itineraries include The American South, Crossroads of America, America's Heartland, and Wilderness Rivers. Cincinnati is one of the departure points, with four-, five-, and seven-night cruises available. Staterooms range from cozy inside cabins to spacious suites; all are decorated with homey prints and antique reproductions. Prices start at about $500 for three-day/two-night getaways. Fares include accommodations, all meals, entertainment, daily activities, and more. For a brochure and more information, call (800) 543–1949 or visit www.deltaqueen.com.

BB Riverboat Tours (ages 2 and up) ⚠

One Madison Avenue, Covington, KY; (800) 261–8586; www.bbriverboats.com. Call for ticket information.

While the *Majestic* stays docked, BB Riverboats still take to the placid waters of the Ohio. Located at Covington Landing across from the baseball stadium, the BB fleet is the city's oldest and largest and offers year-round sightseeing and dining cruises. Enjoy an all-day minivacation cruise, a holiday cruise, or one of the foot-stamping, toe-tapping music, entertainment, and theme cruises. There's even a Skyline Chili Cruise, which features the best of Cincinnati's two famous "skylines"—the real one and the chili. Boats range in size from the modern 580-seat *FunLiner*; an authentic 110-seat stern-wheeler, the *Mark Twain*; and the beautiful, steamboat-era *Becky Thatcher*.

Coney Island (all ages) 🚂

6201 Kellogg Avenue; (513) 232–8230; www.coneyislandpark.com. Call for current hours and rates.

Think Coney Island is in New York? Think again. Cincy is home to this wet-and-wild entertainment complex, located just minutes from downtown at Interstate 275 and Kellogg Avenue. Here you'll find Sunlite, the world's largest recirculating pool; the ZIPP! water coaster; water slides; minigolf; sand volleyball; basketball; bumper boats; pedal boats; skid cars; a tilt-a-whirl; a Ferris wheel; kiddie rides; and more than sixteen classic and family-style rides. Lifeguards even patrol in rubber rafts. The park celebrated its 120th anniversary in 2005.

Cincinnati Zoo and Botanical Garden (all ages) 🐘 🍴 🌼

3400 Vine Street; (513) 281–4700, (800) 94–HIPPO (944–4776); www.cincyzoo.org. Open 365 days a year, 9:00 A.M. to 5:00 P.M., until 6:00 P.M. in summer. Adults $$$, children ages two to twelve $$.

Peacocks have been known to meet and greet guests at the main entrance to the Cincinnati Zoo and Botanical Garden. From I–75 follow the paw prints north of downtown. Here you can check out a population of more than 750 animals. Maybe you'll catch a walrus sleeping on a rock—they turn pink in the sun—or a rare Komodo dragon emerging from its cave (these giant lizards grow to be 10 feet long and weigh

Sexy Cincinnati

The Cincinnati Zoo has been nicknamed "The Sexiest Zoo in America." The park was so dubbed by *Newsweek* magazine because of its successful endangered species reproduction program. Only the zoo in San Diego has a higher success rate in endangered species breeding.

more than 300 pounds!). The zoo's collection of wild cats is said to be the world's most comprehensive, with nineteen different species represented.

Come prepared to spend a leisurely day wandering through one of the top five zoological parks in the nation and one of the most-visited public gardens in the United States. Along the way you'll discover rare wild animals and an extensive and colorful variety of plant life. As the zoo's mission says, "Creating Adventure, Conveying Knowledge, Conserving Nature." The nation's second oldest zoo and a national historic landmark, it is a must-see. More than seventy-five acres house 520 animal species and 3,000 plant varieties.

Early-morning visitors to Gibbon Island are treated to the animals' expressive calls and chatter. On the other side of the park, Wildlife Canyon boasts some of the rarest animals in the zoo's collection, including the delicate Mhorr gazelles, now extinct in the wild; the shy, diminutive zebra duikers; the rare and elusive takin; and the highly endangered Sumatran rhinoceros. A $7.5 million exhibit, Jungle Trails, features two acres of hillside and valley terrain that have been transformed into a lush, Asian/African forest for bonobos (pygmy chimps), orangutans, and smaller primates.

Gorilla World—the lush, tropical home of a lowland gorilla family led by a magnificent silverback male—is home to these gentle giants of the primate kingdom. Other not-to-miss zoo inhabitants include the lovable red pandas, the playful polar bears, and the colorful creatures who flit about in the Butterfly Aviary. Children are encouraged to pet some animals in the Spaulding Children's Zoo as well as take a peek at the adorable animal babies in the zoo's usually crowded nursery. (Zoo babies are also shown off in a festival each spring and a zoo babies' month in June.) The zoo is even fun in the winter, when more than 200 miles of lights cover the grounds, and a Victorian village is centered by an ice-skating rink made of 43,000 pounds of ice.

In 1992 the zoo opened part of its research facility to the public. The $4 million Carl H. Lindner Jr. Family Center for Reproduction of Endangered Wildlife (affectionately known as "CREW") is a modern Noah's ark with fascinating Frozen Zoo and Frozen Garden exhibits. CREW researchers are credited with helping preserve wildlife for generations to come through arrested reproduction techniques. Accomplishments include the world's first successful birth of an exotic animal from a frozen embryo and the first successful interspecies transfer, which resulted in a surrogate eland giving birth to a bonobo. New in 2005 was Wolf Woods, home to Mexican gray wolves, the most endangered subspecies of gray wolf in North America.

After a full day, rest your feet while your kids take a camel ride or enjoy a snack in the Safari restaurant.

Where to Eat

Montgomery Inn, 9440 Montgomery Road; (513) 791–3482. Famous for its barbecue and casual sports bar atmosphere. $–$$

Pomodori's Pizzeria and Trattoria, 121 West McMillen Street; (513) 861–0080. For a lively and inexpensive treat, try this Italian eatery. Pizza is a specialty, and kids get pieces of dough to play with while they wait. $–$$

Rookwood Pottery Restaurant, 1077 Celestial Street; (513) 721–5456. Don't miss the chance to eat in the mammoth kilns that once turned out this avidly collected arts-and-crafts pottery. Casual, with a salad bar and a wide variety of burgers. $$

Where to Stay

Holiday Inn Downtown, 800 West Eighth Street; (513) 241–8660. A popular family choice, this hotel has 244 rooms, a small pool, and an on-site restaurant where kids eat **free** when adult entrees are purchased. $$

Homewood Suites, 2670 East Kemper Road; (513) 772–8888, (800) CALL–HOME (225–5466). A convenient location near Kings Island, **free** breakfast, and large family-size suites with living room, bedroom, and kitchen make this a good bet. $$

Omni Netherlands Plaza, 35 West Fifth Street; (513) 421–9100. This restored 1929 hotel with ornate Art Deco styling is definitely my favorite hotel in Cincy, but it's not cheap. If you're looking to splurge, you won't be disappointed. $$$

For More Information

Greater Cincinnati Convention & Visitors Bureau, (800) CINCY USA (543–2613); www.cincyusa.com.

Southeast Ohio

If you think all of Ohio is flat farmland, think again. The state's many natural wonders can be found in its southeastern region, also known as "Ohio's Outback," where the land is rich with lush forests, splendid waterfalls, and rugged terrain. There are manufactured wonders too: prehistoric earthworks, traditional sternwheelers, picturesque towns, and friendly college campuses that rank among the state's oldest.

Some consider this the most undiscovered part of the state. There are no large cities. Instead, you'll find sleepy, small towns with restored historic districts; country landscapes perfect for family adventures such as hiking, backpacking, or horseback riding; and quiet back roads where you can relax and discover an Ohio unknown to fast-track city residents.

Khristi's
TopPicks for fun in Southeast Ohio

1. Watching endangered wildlife watch us at the Wilds in Cambridge

2. Dude-ranchin' it at Smoke Rise Ranch Resort

3. Exploring Hocking Hills State Park

4. Horseback riding in Shawnee State Forest

5. Going "down on the farm" with Bob Evans in Rio Grande

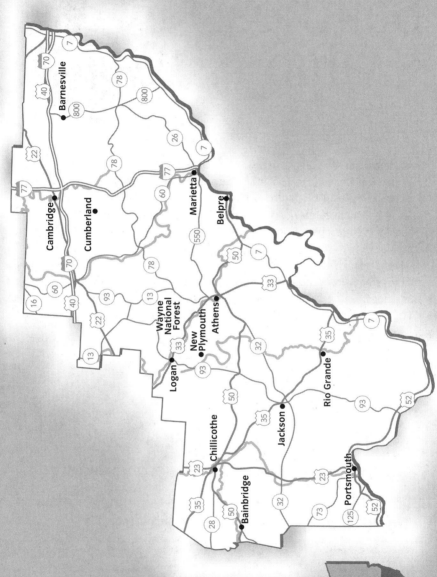

SOUTHEAST OHIO

Barnesville

Cambridge

Cumberland

Marietta

Belpre

Wayne
National
Forest

New
Plymouth

Athens

Logan

Chillicothe

Bainbridge

Jackson

Rio Grande

Portsmouth

Cumberland/Cambridge·

The Wilds (ages 4 and up) 🐘 🍴 🚐 🌿

14000 International Road; (740) 638–5030; www.thewilds.org. Hours vary with the season; call ahead. Closed in winter. Tours: adults $$$, children ages four to twelve $$, under age four **free**. Admission $$, children under age four **free**.

Many of the animals that once roamed Ohio's terrain have long since vanished. It's a fact: Three animal species per day are lost to extinction, and that number is growing rapidly. It's hard to believe that prior to the twentieth century that number was only one species per year. At the current rate, we could lose 20 percent of all species on Earth in the next two decades. It's a sobering thought.

Help your family learn to respect Earth's varied inhabitants with a visit to The Wilds. This expansive preserve, situated on approximately 10,000 acres with rolling grassland, dense forest, and cooling lakes in the northern corner of southeast Ohio, uses state-of-the-art techniques to reproduce and protect many species of vanishing animals. The multimillion-dollar effort, nearly twenty years in the works, is situated on reclaimed mining land. It hopes to help the animals reproduce and survive, with the goal of someday releasing some of the young into their native habitats. With almost 10,000 acres of natural, open-range environment, it's the first preserve of its kind in the world.

Although the preserve has a lofty mission, one of its goals is to make these animals accessible to families who will learn about them by visiting. The two relatively tame African white rhinoceroses in the pen may look ominous, but they're better known as Luanne and Momma, who were moved here from the Columbus Zoo.

Luanne and Momma are just two examples of the endangered species found in this peaceable kingdom. Roaming among the many acres are many animals virtually unknown to today's population, including the Przewalski wild horse from Asia; Hartmann's mountain zebra, of which fewer than 6,000 still survive in southern Africa; the North American red wolf, nearly extinct in the American Southwest; the scimitar-horned oryx; Africa's Cuvier's gazelle, with just 400 in the wild; the Bactrian camel; Jackson's hartebeest; sable and eland antelopes; the reticulated giraffe; and trumpeter and tundra swans. Many of the animals have been given to the facility by zoos that support the preserve's mission and want to see animals in danger of extinction survive.

Visitors see many of these species on the forty-five-minute shuttle tour of the grounds. Few of the animals seem bothered by the buses—some, including a shaggy female Bactrian camel, refuse to move from the road when buses want to get by. A few seem just as curious about their human visitors, craning their necks as the buses roll past.

The Wilds has grown during its eleven-year history into America's largest conservation facility. It's a model to other conservation efforts. Recent attempts to reintroduce ospreys to Ohio have restored these magnificent raptors here to one of their original habitats. They were last seen in the state in the 1940s. Also new, the lodge sleeps up to twelve people and can be rented for an overnight adventure.

Ohio, **Western Style**

Does a Western-style family adventure exist in southeast Ohio? You betcha, pardner. Cowpokes, rustlers, and just regular folks saddle up for getaways at the Smoke Rise Ranch Resort, a working cattle ranch not far from cosmopolitan Athens that offers guests the opportunity to experience Western adventures closer to home. If you saw *City Slickers* and want a taste of that life, this is the vacation for you.

Experience the famed cowboy lifestyle as you and your kids participate in cattle drives, team penning, cow cutting, and guided trail rides. Or, if you prefer, just relax on the more than 2,000 acres of scenic, privately owned land. Located just 7 miles from Burr Oak State Park and bordered by a wildlife management area and the Wayne National Forest, the ranch has places to fish, abundant wildlife, more than 100 miles of well-groomed trails for riding, and more.

The ranch is owned and operated by the Semingson family, who have been in the ranching business all of their lives. As apprentice ranch hands, your family will spend time in the saddle rounding up strays, doctoring sick calves, checking fences, and driving the herd. Guests stay in rustic, bunk-style cabins that sleep up to six people and cook in their cabins or eat in the main dining area. But it's not too rustic; there's also a heated swimming pool, playground, hot tub, and a clubhouse with a kitchen. Activities include pool parties, barbecues, music, and dancing. Smoke Rise also offers a diverse outdoor-education program with a certified naturalist at The Outpost, which has hour-long hikes to weeklong experiences. Parents can enroll their school-age children and enjoy free time for themselves to ride, take lessons, or just relax.

Family weeklong vacations include six nights' cabin accommodations, six days' horse rental, riding lessons, full use of facilities, and other options. Prices range from approximately $1,600 without meals for one person to about $8,000 for a family of six. Weekend vacations with two nights' accommodations are also available, as are overnight stays and camping hookups. For more information write the resort at 6751 Hunterdon, Glouster 45732; (740) 767–2624, (800) 292–1732; www.smokeriseranch.com.

Sure **Thing**

According to Sanford and Joan Portnoy's *How to Take Great Vacations with Your Kids*, favorite family activities while on vacation include (1) heights, (2) water, (3) unusual modes of transportation, (4) animals, and (5) any combination of the above. Keep that in mind when planning the "perfect" family getaway.

Where to Eat

The Forum, 2205 Southgate Parkway; (740) 439–2777. The menu is full of kids' favorites—pizza, burgers, and Italian specialties. $

Where to Stay

Best Western Cambridge, 1945 Southgate Parkway; (740) 439–3581. A hilltop location looks out over the surrounding landscape. The hotel has ninety-five comfortable, if not fancy, rooms. $–$$

Holiday Inn Cambridge, 2248 Southgate Parkway; (740) 432–7313. A handy location, on-site restaurant, and wading pool make this 110-room hotel a good bet for families on the go. $–$$

For More Information

Cambridge/Guernsey County Visitors and Convention Bureau, (800) 933–5480; www.visitguernseycounty.com.

Logan/New Plymouth

Some consider the undulating Hocking Hills to be the state's crown jewels, as well as some of the most un-Ohio-like terrain in Ohio. They're spectacular year-round, with caves, rugged gorges and wooded cliffs, and views that go on for miles, but they're especially breathtaking in the fall, when leaves on the many trees turn varying shades of russet, gold, and scarlet. Located about 15 miles west of Logan, the hills offer a panorama of Ohio geology. Park naturalists like to brag that the Hocking Hills area is a cross between Canada in the valleys and Carolina and Tennessee in the ridges.

The hills are full of superlatives. Here you'll find the state's largest natural rock bridge, its deepest gorge, highest waterfall, and largest recessed cave, all in one area. The scenic valleys and Appalachian foothills in this southeastern Ohio county create a recreational haven where hikers, canoeists, rock climbers, rappelers, equestrians, backpackers, anglers, bicyclists, hunters, birders, or families just out for a breath of fresh air will find a welcome retreat.

Amazing
Ohio Facts

Ohio gained statehood as the seventeenth state in 1803.

Hocking Hills State Park (all ages) 🏛 ❀
19852 Highway 664; (740) 385–6841; www.hockinghillspark.com. Open from dawn to dusk. Free.

Your family will find exciting activities in 2,000-acre Hocking Hills State Park year-round, including sparkling waterfalls and rock formations laden with lore and legend. Follow the trails to Ash Cave, where a 90-foot waterfall marks the spot where Native Americans once camped, and to Old Man's Cave, a former Civil War hermit's haunt and the site of three more stunning cascades and the intriguing rock formation known as the Devil's Bathtub. Junior shutterbugs and family-vacation chroniclers shouldn't miss a shot of the scenic cliffs at Cedar Falls, voted the most photogenic waterfall in the state (you'll also find the state's tallest tree, a 149-foot hemlock), or the observation platform along Rim Trail, with an unsurpassed view of the deep gorge and rare plants that thrive in the strangely named Conkle's Hollow (no one knows who Conkle was, but he left his mark on the gorge: W.J. CONKLE'S 1797). Another must-see: Cantwell Cliffs, with breathtaking 150-foot-high walls (better be in shape—there are hundreds of steps), and the age-old Rock House (where water has slowly carved "rooms" in the side of a cliff), which has a colorful history as a robber's roost (it's also a favorite picnic spot). Rock House was such a popular tourist attraction in the early 1800s that a sixteen-room hotel, complete with ballroom and a U.S. Post Office, was built nearby. You can also rent one of the park's forty heated and air-conditioned family cottages. Call (800) 282–7275 for reservations. For more information on the Hocking Hills area, call (800) HOCKING (462–5464).

Hocking Valley Scenic Railway (all ages)
33 Canal Street, Nelsonville; (740) 753–9531, (800) 967–7834; www.hvsry.org. Two departures daily on weekends from Memorial Day through October. Special Santa trains are offered in December. Routes include a 12-mile trip to Haydenville at noon and a 22-mile trip to Logan at 2:30 P.M. Adults $$, children ages five to twelve $.

All aboard! Another popular attraction in the area is the Hocking Valley Scenic Railway in historic Nelsonville, about thirty minutes away from Hocking Hills State Park. Engine No. 33, a 1916 Baldwin steam locomotive, and a 1950 diesel locomotive offer railway enthusiasts a leisurely ride back in time through the beautiful hills of south-eastern Ohio.

Relive the romance of the rails as the historic locomotives and passenger coaches carry you over century-old tracks through the Wayne National Forest and a right-of-way listed on the National Register of Historic Places, passing brick kilns and a canal lock along the way. Enjoy the blooming dogwood trees in the spring, the lush acreage in the summer, and the spectacular foliage in autumn. There's even a special winter ride with holiday poems, stories, music, and old St. Nick on the Santa Train, a perennial favorite with tiny train buffs (early reservations are recommended).

The train transports visitors through areas not visible from roadways. Trains also stop at Robbins Crossing, an 1860s settler village at Hocking College.

Unique Ohio **Sleepovers**

A Mongolian hut. A traditional tepee. A historic train caboose. An English-style castle. An old-fashioned gypsy wagon. These are just a few of the unusual accommodations that families can enjoy in southeast Ohio's Hocking Hills.

The newly opened Hopping Turtle lets you spend the night alone or with a group in a traditional Sioux tepee. These extraordinary structures measure up to 26 feet across and feature an indoor fire pit. If you're looking for something a bit more conventional, there's also a large four-bedroom home attractively decorated in Native American furnishings. Both are located on fifty wooded acres with miles of hiking trails.

Interested in sleeping in a traditional Mongolian yurt? These circular wooden huts, commonly used by nomads, are covered in vinyl to withstand the elements, yet they offer modern conveniences. Families can gaze through the sun dome at the vast night sky while staying in the large, open-spaced hut.

Other options include a night in an antique red caboose hidden in the woods of the Hocking Hills. The old train caboose has been transformed into a fully equipped cabin with single bunk-style beds that sleep up to five guests, a full kitchen and bath, plus a cozy fire ring just outside the door.

Petite princesses might enjoy a night at Ravenwood Castle, with three accommodation choices, including a cozy reproduction British gypsy wagon equipped with double-decker beds, microwave, and a small refrigerator. Inside the castle, medieval-themed guest rooms offer an enchanted evening.

For more information contact the Hocking Hills Tourism Association at (740) 385–2750 or visit www.1800hocking.com.

Etta's Lunchbox Cafe and General Store 🍴

35960 Highway 56, New Plymouth; (740) 380–0736. Open 10:00 A.M. to 8:00 P.M. Monday through Saturday; 11:00 A.M. to 6:00 P.M. Sunday.

Ohio's Hocking Hills are chock-full of interesting, one-of-a-kind experiences, but LaDora Ousley's Lunchbox Cafe must be one of the best. Named for Ousley's grandmother, it's a unique diner where guests eat surrounded by Ousley's colorful collection of more than 400 lunch boxes. After lunching on homemade diner fare (try the meat loaf or mashed potatoes), be sure to point out to your kids the lunch box you carried to school. Try and stump Ousley, who can identify the year you went to school based on your choice and will be sure to fill you in on interesting background information on that particular lunch box and its production. She'll also tell you what it's worth on the market now, which will have you wishing you'd saved it. Afterward, check out the newer lunch boxes and other goodies for sale in the general store.

"Best of the Road"

The millions of travelers who purchase the *2006 Rand McNally Road Atlas* will discover two of southeast Ohio's "Best of the Road" picks. The Columbus Washboard Factory and Etta's Lunchbox Cafe and General Store were selected by the atlas editors from thousands of unusual destinations across America.

The nation's last remaining company that still manufacturers washboards is located in Ohio's Hocking Hills. The Logan-based company features more than a dozen types of washboards, washboard music kits, and craft ideas. The company has been in business for more than a century and continues to make washboards on turn-of-the-twentieth-century equipment. The company is also the home of a unique folk music festival that celebrates America's Appalachian culture and heritage. The Washboard Music Festival, held each June, draws more than 10,000 visitors from throughout the United States.

Afterward, be sure to stop at Etta's (see listing in this section), a one-time general store launched by LaDora Ousley and named for her grandmother. It features more than 400 lunch boxes from her extensive collection.

For more information on these attractions, visit the area's Web site at www.1800hocking.com.

Mountain Man **Mule Expeditions**

Logan, Highways 46 and 374; (740) 596–1MULE. Prices vary with length of trip.

Ever wanted to ride a pack mule or be a mountain man? In Ohio's Hocking Hills, you'll find your chance. Mountain man wannabe Ken Wells takes visitors on guided mule treks through the remote hollows, caves, and trails of Ohio's breathtaking Hocking Hills.

Where to Stay

Amerihost Inn, 12819 Highway 664, Logan; (740) 385–1700; www.amerihost innlogan.com. Friendly hotel with sixty rooms on the edge of town and near Hocking Hills State Park. There's a pool, sauna, in-room movies, and a free continental breakfast. $–$$

Frontier Log Cabins, 18381 Thompson Ridge Road, Laurelville; (740) 332–6747, (888) 332–6747. Pretend you're a pioneer family during a stay in an original 1800s-era hand-hewn log cabin, restored with a fully equipped kitchen and bath (all you bring are toiletries and food). Located on Hocking County's Skyline Drive, each of the Frontier's log cabins has a fireplace and was constructed of hand-hewn logs from the nearby Hocking Forest. Cabins are located in a secluded area of a forty-year-old white pine forest in Laurelville and are available year-round. $–$$

Hocking Hills State Park Cabins/Campground, Highway 664; (740) 385–6841. The state park rents out forty family-friendly cabins with two bedrooms, bath with shower, fully equipped kitchen with microwave, linens, and a gas fireplace ($$$–$$$$), or you can opt to sleep under the stars in the campgrounds. *NOTE:* Cabins are reserved by the week in summer; fall weekends should be reserved a year in advance. $–$$

Inn at Cedar Falls, 21190 Highway 374, Logan; (740) 385–7489; www.innatcedar falls.com. If you're looking for something truly special, check out these lodgelike cabins at this secluded inn. They're gorgeous—but expensive. Some of the larger ones are suitable for families. $$–$$$

For More Information

Logan County Area Convention and Tourist Bureau, (888) 564–2626; www.logancountyohio.com.

Hocking County Tourism Association, (800) 462–5464; www.hockinghills.com.

Chillicothe

Take U.S. Highway 23 south from Columbus and you'll run directly into Chillicothe, once the capital of Ohio. It's one of the oldest towns in the state, with impressive Victorian-era buildings and long rows of peaceful residential streets. It's a great place to enjoy a relaxing day wandering through the many shops and soaking up the city's long and varied history.

Although the town celebrated its bicentennial in 1996, its history actually began in prehistory, when the area was the home of the mound-building Hopewell and Adena Indians, a culture known as the "Egyptians of the United States" because of the amount of building they did. At one time the Hopewell culture stretched across the United States; many of their burial and ceremonial mounds, however, are found in southern Ohio.

Hopewell Culture National Historic Park (ages 5 and up) 🏛

16062 Highway 104; (740) 774–1125; www.nps.gov/hocu. Open year-round from 8:30 A.M. to 5:00 P.M. $, free for children under seventeen.

The 120-acre Hopewell Culture National Historic Park preserves twenty-three remaining ceremonial mounds and runs an innovative Junior Ranger program for kids that teaches them about the park and the long-ago people who built it.

A free Junior Ranger booklet guides families through the highlights of the park, including an on-site museum and visitor center. While in the visitor center, don't miss the award-winning *Legacy of the Moundbuilders,* a fifteen-minute video that recounts the lives and lore of the Hopewell. There's also a well-stocked bookstore with books on archaeology and Native American culture for adults and children.

After visiting, kids are encouraged to fill out the questionnaire in the Junior Ranger booklet; they're then "sworn in" as honorary Junior Rangers, complete with badge.

Tecumseh! (ages 5 and up) 🎵 🚻 🍴

Sugarloaf Mountain Amphitheatre, Delano Road off Highway 159; (740) 775–0700; www.tecumsehdrama.com. Offered June through August only. Adults $$$, children ages ten and younger $$.

Southeast Ohio's earliest days are also the subject of *Tecumseh!,* a spectacular reenactment of the life and times of the great Shawnee leader. A large, tiered amphitheater nestled in the hardwood forest of Sugarloaf Mountain has become a mecca for more than a million tourists annually from all over the world who come to sit among birds and forest and be carried back through time to another world.

The show has earned accolades from around the country: "Easily the most massive and impressive outdoor spectacle east of the Mississippi," says the *Richmond Times-Dispatch;* "It ought to be required viewing for every schoolchild in Ohio," claims the *Troy Daily News.*

Here, under the stars, kids watch wide-eyed as horses gallop down from the hills, arrows wing overhead, and artillery thunders through the surrounding country. At any time, cross fire threatens half the audience. Although the performance has been occasionally criticized for taking "literary license" with history, it's a sure way to get your children interested in the lives of men and women who lived and died long ago.

Another sure hit with families is the backstage tour, offered daily except Sunday at 4:00 and 5:00 P.M. Cast members serve as guides, providing a historical background of the area and theater before leading visitors backstage through the lighting, set, props, techniques, and pyrotechnics. As part of the tour, the stuntmen give lively displays of stage combat and flintlock firing, and even pitch headfirst from a 21-foot cliff. Afterward, they get up and explain how they did it to a fascinated, adoring crowd. Tours $.

There's also a **free** prehistoric Native American minimuseum, with artifacts from the first settlers of Ohio Country; a restaurant overlooking a vista of forests and mountains, featuring a popular buffet from 4:30 to 7:45 P.M. each evening (adults $$, children ages ten and younger $; reservations required); and the Mountain Valley gift shop, across from the box office, with handcrafted Native American jewelry, pottery, and other gifts and souvenirs.

Bed, Breakfast, **and Baby**

We know all the pluses of a chain hotel—a pool where the kids can work off their excess energy, anonymity (no one will know that it was your fourteen-month-old who screamed all night because of an ear infection), and reasonable rates. But as your kids get older or you become tired of cookie-cutter chains, one option makes traveling a bit more, well, welcoming.

More and more bed-and-breakfasts are responding to the growing family market by opening their historic doors to children of all ages. During a recent stay at the Twin Oaks Inn in Saugatuck, Michigan, my brood was treated as adopted nieces and nephews. There was a basket full of well-loved toys, a roll-away crib in the room, and a library of videos for movie fans of all ages. There's even a resident "Grandma" (the owner's mother) who oversees the property and passes out hugs. Only drawback: She doesn't baby-sit.

Interested? Chambers of commerce or convention and visitors bureaus are good sources for a list of bed-and-breakfasts in a specific area.

Where to Eat

Carl's Townhouse, 95 South Paint Street; (740) 773–1660. The motto of this tiny, authentic 1930s diner is "A Clean Place to Eat." This neighborhood joint is where families come in for the justly famous single, double, or triple hamburgers and homemade soups such as bean and vegetable, and where regulars still tally up their own bill. $–$$

New York, New York, 200 North Plaza Boulevard; (740) 773–2100. Small, family-friendly eatery features a relaxed atmosphere and kid favorites such as pizza and pastas. $–$$

Where to Stay

Christopher Inn, 30 North Plaza; (740) 774–6835. This pleasant, country-style inn has sixty-one rooms, complimentary evening beverages, a deluxe continental breakfast for hungry kids, and a heated indoor pool. $–$$

Days Inn, 1250 North Bridge Road; (740) 775–7000. Features 142 rooms, some with a whirlpool. $–$$

Hampton Inn & Suites, 100 North Plaza Boulevard; (740) 773–1616. Has spacious rooms and suites near a quiet park. More than twenty rooms have a handy kitchenette. Pool, sauna, too. $–$$

Bainbridge

Seven Caves (ages 4 and up)

7660 Cave Road; (937) 365–1283. Open 9:00 A.M. to dark daily year-round. Adults $$, children ages five to eleven $.

Bring the hiking boots when you head out for a visit to the Seven Caves. West of Bainbridge off U.S. Highway 50, Seven Caves makes spelunkers' fantasies come true. Lace up and follow the three nature trails into the caves, where you'll find cement walks, handrails, and push-button lighting that emphasizes formations along the way. Cliffs, canyons, waterfalls, and more than 300 species of plants and trees are found in the adjacent park.

Where to Eat

Market Square Bistro, 16715 Chillicothe Road; (937) 543–5115. A noisy and fun casual eatery with wood floors and huge portions of kid-pleasing favorites such as burgers and pasta. $

Portsmouth

Shawnee State Park (all ages) ⬤⬤⬤

13291 U.S. Highway 52, West Portsmouth; (740) 858–6685; www.dnr.state.oh/us. Open 6:00 A.M. to 11:00 P.M. Free.

This Ohio River town is the gateway to Shawnee State Park, also known as Ohio's "Little Smokies." Nestled in the Appalachian foothills on the banks of the Ohio River, the state park comprises a dramatically hilly wilderness area of nearly 62,000 acres of unbroken land. It's the largest contiguous forest in the state, with so many trees that a constant blue haze seems to hang in the air, giving the park an ethereal, otherworldly feeling.

Partaking of worldly pleasures such as horseback riding and backpacking is the best way to see the park. In spring the hillsides are splashed with wildflowers; in fall a spectacular spray of colors brightens the vista. You also can drive your car along the 170 miles of roadway that are maintained by the Division of Forestry. If you do nothing else, don't miss the Panoramic Scenic Loop Drive for its route through the forest and its unforgettable overlooks.

Southern Ohio Museum and Cultural Center (ages 5 and up) ⬤

825 Gallia Street; (740) 354–5629. $2.00 adults, $1.00 children; free on Friday.

The distant past and the life of the Mound Builders come alive in a new exhibition at the Southern Ohio Museum in Portsmouth. The museum's new permanent exhibit features more than 10,000 Native American artifacts that range from 1,500 to 8,000 years old and depict the rich, unwritten story of the ancient native people known as the Mound Builders. Downtown Portsmouth also sits on the former location of numerous mounds. Artifacts in the exhibit come almost exclusively from ancient village sites in the Ohio River Valley.

Where to Eat

Johnson's Seafood Restaurant, 2828 Gallia Street; (740) 353–1765. Casual eatery with a good children's menu and seafood specialties. $–$$

Where to Stay

Best Western, 3762 U.S. Highway 23 N; (740) 353–2084. Cheerful hotel with one hundred rooms and a cozy, country decor make this a good bet for families. $–$$

Shawnee Resort and Conference Center, US 52; (800) AT–A–PARK (282–7275); www.shawneelodgeresort. Although camping is available at the park's deluxe facility (there are 107 sites), many guests opt to stay in the fifty-room Shawnee Resort and Conference Center, opened in 1973. While stocked with modern conveniences, the lodge has a rustic, Native American flavor that families find irresistible. Big stone fireplaces, timber framing, arrow and spear collections, and a full-size birch-bark canoe add to the ambience. Guest rooms sport furnishings crafted by local artisans.

The lodge's outdoor pool and sundeck have a great view of Turkey Foot Lake and the park's ragged ridges. There are also an indoor pool, whirlpool, sauna, and exercise room. Rooms—many with vaulted ceilings and pine walls—are spacious and feature Native American designs and nature posters. The lodge also has twenty-five family cabins on a ridge near the lodge. There's an eighteen-hole championship golf course adjacent to the Ohio River, as well as fishing, boating, tennis, a game room, and hayrides. $$–$$$

Tepee **Time**

Rent-A-Tepee is available at three Ohio state park locations throughout the state. Camping gear is provided, along with use of a canoe for an unusual family camping adventure. For more information call (800) AT–A–PARK (282–7275) or write the Ohio State Parks Information Center at 1952 Belcher Drive, Building C-3, Columbus 43224-1386.

Rio Grande

Bob Evans Farm (all ages) 🍴 🔺 ❌ 🏠
Highway 588 just off U.S. Highway 35; (800) 994–FARM (3276); www.bobevans.com. Open 9:00 A.M. to 5:00 P.M. daily from Memorial Day weekend through Labor Day, as well as weekends in September. $

Your family has eaten the sausage a hundred times, but did you know that Bob Evans was a real person? And that he really did live "down on the farm"?

The one-thousand-acre Bob Evans Farm in Rio Grande, not far from the West Virginia border, was home to Bob Evans, founder of Bob Evans Farms, for nearly twenty years. Bob and his wife, Jewel, raised their six children in the large, 1820s-era brick farmhouse known as the Homestead. A former stagecoach stop and inn, the house is now listed on the National Register of Historic Places. The Homestead Museum, the latest addition, opened in May 2003.

It was here that Bob first made the sausage that would make him famous. In 1946 he whipped up a batch for the twelve-stool, twenty-four-hour restaurant he had opened in nearby Gallipolis. As a sideline, he sold ten-pound tubs of sausage to restaurant patrons, eventually expanding his distribution to nearby grocery stores. As his popularity grew, Bob invited clients to come "down on the farm" to see where the sausage was made.

As more and more people came, however, he decided to open a little sausage shop. The Sausage Shop, which is now a Bob Evans Restaurant, was the company's first venture into the restaurant business.

After a hearty breakfast at the restaurant (the biscuits are second to none), grab a paddle and head for Raccoon Creek (really a river, but the old name stuck), where the waters are blue-green and make for adventurous canoeing. Or saddle up for a spin around the farm via horseback. Want to stay on terra firma? The barnyard has a passel of friendly farm animals that love to be petted.

While there, take a hike among the farm's 1,000 acres of rolling hills or peruse the museum of farm implements and farm life. An authentic log cabin provides insights into a bygone way of life. And if you're here in October, don't miss the annual Bob Evans Farm Festival, with more than one hundred craftspeople and country entertainment (including apple-peeling, corn-shelling, a feed-sack race, a cow-chip throwing contest, and hog-calling), as well as tractor pulls, wagon rides, and—of course—plenty of food.

Where to Stay

College Hill Motel, 10987 Highway 588; (740) 245–5326. A small and simple hotel with clean, modest rooms and a nearby restaurant. Rooms have free movies. $

World's Largest **Basket**

Dresden, a sleepy 1950s village, is fast becoming the basket-weaving capital of the world. Here, the Longaberger Company has produced beautiful handmade baskets for more than sixty years. The baskets have recently become a favorite of collectors, who come here to watch them as they're being made. While in town, check out the Longaberger Gallery at the corner of Main and Fifth Streets downtown, home to the World's Largest Basket. Made of ten hard maples, it took 2,000 hours to complete. It measures 48 feet long, 11 feet wide, and 23 feet high.

Marietta

Westward, Ho! In many ways, the U.S. westward expansion began with the establishment of the city of Marietta. This southern Ohio city—locally known as "The Riverboat City"—was the first organized American settlement in the Northwest Territory and the state's "first" city. The original forty-seven pioneers of the Ohio Company arrived in Marietta from New England by flatboat in 1788. Many of the settlers were veteran officers of the Revolutionary War who received land in lieu of cash for their wartime services. Farsighted and community-minded, they designed wide streets lined with beautiful homes as well as parks and common areas. In honor of Queen Marie Antoinette of France, they named the city Marietta.

Luckily, the city has enjoyed a better fate than its namesake. Today many of those historic sites remain and many more attractions have been added, making Marietta one of the state's most charming and fascinating destinations. In many ways it appears as if a little bit of New England has been transplanted to the Ohio prairie.

Classic Carriage Rides (all ages)

101 Front Street; (740) 667–3513. Rides depart from the front of the Lafayette Hotel on Friday and Saturday nights. $$; children ride free.

For an up-close view of the city, consider a ride in a vintage horse-drawn carriage. Classic Carriage takes families back in time as they clip-clop down brick-lined streets through the historic city.

Historic Harmar Village (all ages)

220 Gilman Street; (740) 374–9995; www.harmarvillage.com. Open 11:00 A.M. to 5:00 P.M. daily. $, free for children under ten.

Train buffs love the quaint shops and restaurants here, but the highlight is definitely Harmar Station, where more than 250 train models are displayed. Some two dozen operate continuously, a delight for small children.

Trolley Tours (all ages)

127 Ohio Street; (740) 374–2233. Trips are offered April through October. Adults $$, children ages five to twelve $.

Although not quite as old a means of transportation, the city's Trolley Tours are loads of fun. Hop on board one of these beauties and, with the clang-clang of the bell, you're off on a narrated tour that takes in all the city's highlights, including the Victorian-style shops along Front Street, Marietta College, and more. Call for schedules and more information.

Campus Martius Museum (ages 3 and up)

601 Second Street; (740) 373–3750, (800) 860–0145; www.ohiohistory.org. Open Wednesday through Saturday from 9:30 A.M. to 5:00 P.M. and Sunday from noon to 5:00 P.M. Adults $$, students six to twelve $.

Today the Campus Martius Museum sits on the site of the city's original fortification. Newly restored, it preserves the history of Marietta, early Ohio, and the Northwest Territory. With original pioneer artifacts, original maps, tools, furnishings, agricultural implements, and even a full-size home, it preserves a way of life long since past in the state. If your kids have only seen covered Conestoga wagons in television westerns, here's your chance to show them the real thing.

The full-size home once belonged to Rufus Putnam, superintendent of the Ohio Company of Associates, the landholders responsible for Marietta's settlement. You can't help but wander through the rooms of the simple, plank structure and wonder at the hard lives of the people who once lived here or what the walls have seen and heard. The oldest home in the state, the house still stands in its original location and is the only surviving dwelling of the original fortification. The land office of the Ohio Company, from which portions of the land were divvied up, is also housed here. The newest exhibit, Paradise Found and Lost: Migration in Ohio Valley 1850–1970, documents the area's migratory history.

Children's Toy and Doll Museum (ages 2 and up)

206 Gilman Street; (740) 373–1168; www.harmarvillage.com. Open noon to 4:00 P.M. Saturday and Sunday year-round. Admission by donation.

History of another kind is found at the city's charming Children's Toy and Doll Museum. Located in a restored B&O passenger train car in historic Harmar Village, it's a family favorite and a surefire hit with younger children. Three of the most enchanting highlights include the talking dollhouse, which tells the story of a Christmas wedding circa 1900; the Cook Dollhouse, which contains miniatures from all over the world; and the Betsy Ross Dollhouse, built the day after she made America's first flag. Can't wait till Christmas? Get ready for Santa with a trip to his workshop, where tiny elves work around the clock to get ready for that special day. Also found here are Marietta's first teddy bear, baby dolls, games and collections, and a host of other old beloved toys.

Butch's Cola Museum (ages 5 and up)

118 Maple Street; (740) 376–COKE (2653); www.harmarvillage.com. Hours vary with the season. $, free for kids.

You know it's the real thing, but did you know that there's a whole museum devoted to Coca-Cola? In the years since Butch's Cola Museum has been in existence, it has attracted collectors and the curious from all fifty states as well as sixty-six foreign countries. Located in Harmar Village, the museum chronicles the rise (and rise and rise) of this beloved soft drink. Butch started collecting Coke memorabilia almost twenty years ago. As his collection took off, he moved it to the museum, where it now spotlights memorabilia from 1900 to the present. The collection includes signs, coolers, machines, and paper items that he's accumulated over the years, including a rare 1900 Icy-O cooler, one of only six remaining in the world. There's also a gift shop and a model of an old country store.

Ohio River Sternwheel Festival (all ages)

316 Third Street; (800) 288–2577.

Steamboatin' plays a large part in the city's history and psyche. One of the city's liveliest events is the Ohio River Sternwheel Festival, held for three days each September. Marietta is home of the American Sternwheel Association and the rightful host of this annual event.

Included in the festivities is entertainment from calliope to jazz, the crowning of Queen Genevieve of the River during a headliner concert, and a dazzling fireworks display. Sunday brings riverside church services and the grand finale: the colorful, hard-fought stern-wheel races.

Ohio River Museum (ages 4 and up)

601 Second Street; (740) 373–3717, (800) 860–0145; www.ohiohistory.org. Hours vary; closed October 31 through end of May. Adults $$, children ages six to twelve $, and free for children under six.

For a lively account of the stern-wheel's history, check out the Ohio River Museum on Front Street. It chronicles the exciting era in which elegant steamboats and floating hotels plied the Ohio.

After the Civil War, however, railroads cut into the steamboats' profits. Quicker speeds, better cargo handling, and easier scheduling enticed travelers and businesses to switch allegiance to the new mode of transportation. Soon, the less-efficient steamboats were all but retired from the river.

Today remnants of that proud past can be found preserved in museums. The one in Marietta, opened in 1974, is one of the best and most comprehensive. A good first stop is the full-size diorama that re-creates the wildlife found along an Ohio waterway two centuries ago. A thirty-minute video on steamboat history entitled *Fire on the Water* explores the often-dangerous days when boilers were known to explode, killing hundreds (rest assured—most of today's steamboats are diesel-powered and driven by propellers while a fake stern-wheel is moved by the passing water), and contains footage of both old excursion boats and present-day steamboats such as the *Delta Queen*.

Here you'll also find one of the oldest existing steamboat pilothouses, from the *Tell City*, built in 1885. Kids will get a kick out of standing behind the wooden wheel and pretending they're the captain piloting the boat down the river. Along with scaled-down riverboat models, ornate cabin furnishings, and other memorabilia from the golden age of steamboat travel, the museum offers a full-size example, the *W. P. Snyder,* the sole surviving steam-powered stern-wheel towboat in the United States. Another crowd-pleaser is the school of carp that takes up summer residence beside the towboat *W. P. Snyder Jr.* in order to feed on the bread that visitors throw. The carp—like the swallows at San Juan Capistrano—are so faithful to the locale that they return each April.

Valley Gem Stern-wheeler (all ages)

601 Front Street; (740) 373–7862; www.valleygemsternwheeler.com. Hour-long narrated tours: adults $$, children ages two to twelve $. Dinner cruises are held on Saturday evening with a buffet meal. There are also special three- to four-hour fall-foliage tours on weekends in October (adults $$$, kids $$). Call for times and more information.

If you'd love to ride one of these beauties, a number of local companies offer riverboat excursions along the Ohio and Muskingum Rivers. From May through November your family can enjoy a ride on the 300-seat *Valley Gem* stern-wheeler, a Coast Guard–approved authentic stern-wheeler built in 1988. With its big paddle wheel churning up the river, it's a slice of Americana you won't find anywhere else. George H. W. Bush even dropped by once for a ride during a presidential campaign visit. It docks at the Washington Street Landing, under the bridge and adjacent to the Ohio River Museum.

Showboat Becky Thatcher (ages 5 and up) 🎵

347 Front Street; (740) 350–4133, (877) SHO–BOAT (746–2628); www.marietta-ohio .com/beckythatcher.

Another vintage stern-wheeler, the *Becky Thatcher*, attracts hundreds of passengers but never leaves port. With parts built in the 1890s and the 1920s, she once plied the Mississippi and Ohio Rivers and hosted three presidents during a stint as an Army Corps boat used for visiting dignitaries. She ended up in Marietta after being towed thousands of miles for the city's bicentennial celebration and never left.

Today she's known as the *Showboat Becky Thatcher.* The old boiler room has become a theater where talent from all over the country entertains crowds in lively melodramas such as *Little Mary Sunshine* and one-man plays including *Ring, Ring the Banjo: An Evening with Stephen Foster.* (Foster, for the uninitiated, was the composer of such classics as "Oh Susanna," "Camptown Races," and "My Old Kentucky Home.") Villains, heroes, and heroines are introduced to the audience at the beginning of the performance; placards even instruct you when to boo and cheer.

Where to Eat

Becky Thatcher Restaurant, *Showboat Becky Thatcher;* (740) 350–4133. The upper deck of this historic stern-wheeler houses the Becky Thatcher Restaurant, featuring an enthusiastic waitstaff serving steak, chicken, seafood, and a dessert known as Riverboat pie, made with coffee ice cream and other secret ingredients. Kids love it, too. $$

The Gun Room, 101 Front Street; (740) 373–5522. Located in the historic Lafayette Hotel, this casual restaurant has a riverboat theme and a popular children's menu. Get there early and you can take advantage of the well-priced "early-bird spe-

cials." There's also an extensive lunch buffet. $–$$

Levee House Cafe, 127 Ohio Street; (740) 374–2234. Bright, cheery cafe with alfresco dining in season, seafood dishes, and imaginative pasta specials. $–$$

Where to Stay

Best Western Marietta, 279 Muskingum Drive; (740) 374–7211. All the hotel's forty-seven rooms on the Muskingum River have refrigerators, a plus for parents laden with snacks and drinks. Some of the rooms are two-bedroom units perfect for families. $–$$

Comfort Inn Marietta, 700 Pike Street; (740) 374–8190. Free coffee gets high marks from tired parents, and the kids like the 121-room hotel's free movies. $

For More Information

Marietta/Washington County Convention & Visitors Bureau, (800) 288–2577; www.mariettaohio.org.

Rooms **at the Inn**

Most hotels will let you see your room before you pay for it. Test the beds, check out the bathroom, and see how far it is to the pool. If you don't like where they put you, ask for another room.

Belpre

Lee Middleton Original Doll Factory (ages 2 and up)

1301 Washington Boulevard; (740) 423–1481, (800) 233–7479; www.leemiddleton.com. Tours are offered hourly Monday through Friday from 9:00 A.M. to 3:00 P.M. except during January and February. Lee Middleton dolls also are found in shops throughout the state. **Free.**

It's only fitting that the Lee Middleton Original Doll Factory on Washington Boulevard looks like a giant dollhouse, complete with fancy gingerbread trim. Inside, big and little enthusiasts alike watch with fascination as the highly collectible and incredibly realistic dolls created by sculptor Lee Middleton Urick are made right before their eyes. Urick began sculpting dolls at her kitchen table and was the first original doll artist to build and manage a major manufacturing facility to create her work.

The company relocated its headquarters to Columbus a few years ago because of unprecedented growth and the death of the founder. Today, the factory, nursery, and gift shop remain in the original location.

Afterward, try and resist a visit to the nursery, where you can adopt a life-size Middleton baby (they wear real birth-to-three-month-size baby clothes!), complete with papers, promises, and pictures. All dolls are signed and numbered. The company even makes officially licensed dolls for Hershey's, including two known as "Hershey's Kisses" dressed in gold and silver lamé. Don't miss the 37,000-square-foot, life-size dollhouse with gingerbread trim.

Prices for the latest Middleton creation can reach into the thousands. Collectors and children looking for something a little less expensive should check out the less-than-perfect section in the gift shop, where dolls have minor flaws undetectable to the layman, or the bargain "store editions" that are put together with leftover outfits and materials.

Amazing
Ohio Facts

The population of Ohio is approximately 11,459,011 (2004).

The capital of Ohio is Columbus.

Barnesville

Barbara Barbe Doll Museum (ages 2 and up)

211 North Chestnut Street; (740) 425–2301. Open from 1:00 to 4:00 P.M. Wednesday through Sunday from May 1 through September 30; tours are by appointment year-round. $, **free** for children under six.

This peaceful town was settled by the Quakers in the early 1800s and has a well-preserved historic district. Most little girls, however, care only for the Barbara Barbe Doll Museum, stuffed to the rafters with hundreds of beguiling nineteenth- and twentieth-century dolls.

Five rooms in a former 1836 women's seminary make up the small museum, which displays more than 800 of the 3,500 dolls collected by former Barnesville resident Barbe. When she died, her three sons were at a loss as to what to do with the collection. Today it attracts thousands of doll collectors, crafters, and enthusiastic little girls who ooh and aah over the German, French, and American bisque dolls; dolls from around the world (most dressed in original costumes); and the extensive Barbie Doll collection, which takes up one whole room.

For More Information

Barnesville Area Chamber of Commerce, (740) 425–4300; www.barnesvilleohio.com.

Athens

Home of Ohio University, Athens is a pleasing mix of Appalachia and academia tucked into the hills of southeast Ohio. The brick streets of "uptown" Athens pulsate with the energy of more than 18,000 students, with lively shops and eateries that cater to young tastes and interests. Although urbane in many senses, it's also the gateway to the coal country of West Virginia and an entryway to the nearby Wayne National Forest. A pleasing mix of country and city, there are places to buy both sushi and sickles.

To Camp or **Not to Camp**

Thinking about camping out? If your family consists of first-timers, consider renting or borrowing equipment and testing it over a long weekend before you invest time and money in a longer adventure. There's nothing worse than whiny kids and rainy weather when there's a Holiday Inn down the street.

Hockhocking Adena Bikeway (all ages) 🚲
667 East State Street; (800) 878–9767.

Stretching between Nelsonville and Athens, the 17-mile Hockhocking Adena Bikeway gets its unusual name from a Native American word for "twisted," a reference to the Hocking River. The ancient Adena Indians once inhabited the surrounding hills; today the area is better known for its variety of geographical features. The bikeway flanks both the Wayne National Forest and the Ohio University campus in Athens. It's open to bikes, hikers, in-line skaters, and wheelchairs, but not to horseback riders.

Southeastern Ohio Cultural Arts Center (ages 4 and up) 🏛
8000 Dairy Lane; (740) 592–4981; www.dairybarn.org. **Open Wednesday through Sunday from 11:00 A.M. to 5:00 P.M., Thursday to 8:00 P.M. Adults $, free for kids under twelve, and free for all on Thursday evening.**

Athens is also home to the Southeastern Ohio Cultural Arts Center, more affectionately known as the Dairy Barn. Not surprisingly, the 1914 barn was once part of a dairy farm, part of the Athens Asylum, where patients milked cows as part of their therapy. A community arts center in the truest sense, today the spacious center attracts the crème de la crème of national and international folk art. It features four to five exhibitions in 6,500 feet of gallery space each year. Quilt National, held every other summer, attracts thousands of entries and visitors annually. The yearly children's holiday festival features hayrides, storytellers, crafts, and more.

Wayne National Forest (all ages) 🚶🍽🎣🛶⛺
13700 U.S. Highway 33; (740) 753–0101; www.fs.fed.us/r9/wayne/.

Encompassing an area of more than 200,000 acres spread out across several southeastern counties, the vast Wayne National Forest is the state's only national forest. There are plenty of free opportunities for camping, hiking, picnicking, fishing, horseback riding, and even specially marked trails for off-road vehicles, something not found in other area parks. Elevations in the forest range from 630 feet on the Ohio River to 1,320 feet on the Narrows River.

Like ghost towns? Along the hiking trails are remnants of abandoned cabin and homestead sites and other eerie signs of former inhabitants. You'll also pass the remains of a one-room schoolhouse, an oil well, and an abandoned farmhouse. Year-round you'll find evidence of the abundant wildlife and plant life that characterize this beautiful and rugged land. And if you'd like to pitch a tent and sleep under the stars, no permits are necessary, although state licenses are required for hunting, fishing, and gathering firewood.

Where to Eat

Lui-Lui Restaurant, 8 Station Street; (740) 594–8905. Friendly, casual cafe featuring Thai and Chinese dishes as well as popular brick-oven pizzas. Smoke-free. $

Sylvia's Restaurant, 4 Depot Street; (740) 594–3484. Italian eatery known for its wide selection of pastas and seafood and well-priced children's menu. $–$$

Zacharay's Specialty Deli, 30 North Court Street; (740) 592–2000. Relaxed, deli-style restaurant with a wide variety of favorites and a children's menu. $

Where to Stay

Amerihost Inn, 20 Home Street; (740) 594–3000. The hotel's 102 rooms are located near a shopping center and jogging path along the Hocking River. All rooms have coffeemakers and free movies; some have microwaves, refrigerators, and whirlpools. $–$$

Days Inn, 330 Columbus Road; (740) 592–4000. Clean and inexpensive budget hotel with sixty rooms and free movies. $

Ohio University Inn and Conference Center, 331 Richland Avenue; (740) 593–6661. Adjacent to campus, with 139 rooms, a nearby public park, dining room, and free movies. $–$$

For more information

Athens Country Convention and Visitors Bureau, (800) 878–9767; www.athensohio.com.

Tried and **True Tip**

When traveling (especially in winter), look for hotels with heated indoor pools.

Fun Family **Festivals**

Ohio is home to many fun, family-style festivals and exciting annual events. Here are a few worth checking out the next time you're in the area.

Maple Syrup Festival, Lucas. Malabar Farm Park is the place for demonstrations of early Native American and modern sugaring techniques as well as self-guided tours. Learn about the evolution of sap to syrup while enjoying free samples and entertainment. March.

River City Ohio Blues Festival, Marietta. Music lovers from across the country descend on Marietta for this three-day celebration of toe-tapping blues music. Nationally known performers take the stage as well as winners of the River City Ohio Blues Competition. March.

Hopalong Cassidy Festival, Cambridge. Justice, gallantry, and bravery ride again at this festival honoring an American legend. Enjoy continuous entertainment, free movies, a collectors' show, a Western parade, a little buckaroo and cowboy look-alike contest, and the chance to meet stars from old Western movies. May.

International Migratory Bird Day, Oak Harbor. Held for only two days each year, this event kicks off the spectacular birding season. Bird displays, guided bird hikes, and other family activities attract visitors of all ages. May.

Dulcimer Days, Roscoe Village. Lively melodies and workshops as well as the Mid-Eastern Regional Dulcimer Championships at Historic Roscoe Village attract families and fans. Sit back and listen to great music, or bring your instruments and strum along. May.

Dublin Irish Festival, Dublin. Irish eyes are smilin' during this annual event, which features some of the world's best Celtic musicians, step dancers, and artisans. There's also an Irish marketplace, the Wee Folk children's area, hands-on cultural workshops, and genealogists to trace family roots. August.

Melon Festival, Milan. Milan celebrates its melons, famous for their delicious sweet flavor and superb quality, with a parade, melon ice cream, carnival rides, and games. August.

Johnny Appleseed Festival, Defiance. Step back in time as village craftspeople demonstrate their pioneer skills. Kids can help make apple butter and molasses, tour the twenty-two village buildings and seven nearby museums, and more. October.

Wildlights, Columbus. More than two million lights and 200 lighted ground displays illuminate the park in December. Fun family activities, including ice skating, horse-drawn wagon rides, and visits with Santa are part of the fun. There's also a special tribute to Kwanzaa, where families can learn more about the traditions, crafts, and music and dance. November and December.

Christmas Candlelighting, Coshocton. Historic Roscoe Village celebrates the holidays all month long with its candlelighting festivities. Travelers to the historic canal town enjoy shopping, caroling, cookies, and visits with Santa. The activities kick off with the lighting of the tree in the old-fashioned town square. December.

Jackson

Noah's Ark Animal Farm (all ages) 🐘 ⚠️ 🐱 🔒

1527 McGiffins Road; (740) 384–3060, (800) 282–2167. Open Monday through Saturday from 10:00 A.M. to 6:00 P.M. and Sunday from noon to 7:00 P.M. The recreation area is open April 1 through December 15; the farm area is open April 1 through October 30. Adults $$, children ages three to twelve $.

If huge zoos and theme parks are too much for your preschoolers, Noah's Ark Animal Farm may be the answer. Located on Highway 32 southwest of Athens, it's home to more than 150 exotic animals and birds. The small-scale park was the dream of a local businessman and his wife who traveled around the country with their sons. Along the way they stopped at and were inspired by small animal and theme parks in Pennsylvania and Wisconsin.

Later they combined their love of animals, railroads, farming, and golfing into this thirty-five-acre farm. Today kids from all over the country are enchanted by the chance to view and feed the animals (North American black bears, cougars, raccoons, pygmy goats, llamas, wild turkeys, and more), ride the ¾-mile loop on the antique miniature train, shoot a round of eighteen-hole miniature golf, or burn off some steam in the playground. You also can build up your muscles on the paddleboats ($ per half hour); fish at Pay Lake, which is stocked weekly; or toss a horseshoe or two at the recreation area ($).

Where to Eat

Lewis Family Restaurant, 966 East Main Street; (740) 286–5413. Turkey is a local favorite, as are the extensive salad bar and stacked sandwiches. $–$$

Where to Stay

Comfort Inn, 605 East Main Street; (740) 286–7581. Cozy hotel with fifty-two rooms, many with sleeper sofas. Free movies. $

General Index

Activities Index

Events/Festivals

Farms/Ranches

Historic Sites and Villages

Museums

Nature Centers/ Animal Preserves

Parks, Recreation Areas

About the Author

Khristi Sigurdson Zimmeth is an award-winning writer and editor based in Grosse Pointe Park, Michigan. Besides writing travel books, she is senior editor of *Michigan Living* magazine, the state's largest magazine. When not exploring the world on business trips, she enjoys traveling with her husband, John, and two children, Nate and Claire. A gardening and home-design enthusiast, she also serves as a regional editor for *Better Homes and Gardens* and the magazine's various garden and design publications.

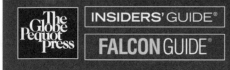